Sewing Cozy Craft Projects

Make Adorable Animal Décor, Gifts, and Keepsakes

Olesya Lebedenko

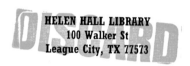

Landauer Publishing

Sewing Cozy Craft Projects

Landauer Publishing, www.landauerpub.com, is an imprint of Fox Chapel Publishing Company, Inc.

© 2021 by Olesya Lebedenko and Fox Chapel Publishing Company, Inc., 903 Square Street, Mount Joy, PA 17552.

Project Team
Editor: Amy Deputato
Copy Editor: Hayley DeBerard
Designer: Llara Pazdan
Photographers: Mike Mihalo, cover and glamor photography; Olesya Lebedenko, all photos not otherwise credited
Images from www.Shutterstock.com: photonova (59, 4, 12, 13, 88); Eky Studio (35, 41, 45, 53, 57); Vitolga (7 bottom right); Rudenko Roman (small line art graphics throughout)

ISBN 978-1-947163-70-6

Library of Congress Control Number: 2021935568

We are always looking for talented authors. To submit an idea, please send a brief inquiry to acquisitions@foxchapelpublishing.com.

Printed in Singapore
24 23 22 21   2 4 6 8 10 9 7 5 3 1

Contents

Acknowledgments

To my marvelous editors, Amelia Johanson and Amy Deputato: How can I ever thank you enough for making my books better? And how can I ever thank you enough for the e-mails, reminders, and patience? I don't think I would have enjoyed this "pieceful" journey half as much without you.

These books would not exist without the hardworking teams at Landauer and Fox Chapel Publishing, so my eternal respect and gratitude go to Kerry Bogert, David Miller, and all the designers, editors, and photographers.

To BERNINA Canada: Thank you for the sponsorship and incredible support! This book would never have been finished on time without the B 475 and the special binder attachment.

To my husband, Nazar: You inspire and challenge me not only to be a better designer and quilter but also to be a better person. Your love and friendship give me strength, courage, and hope. No matter what happens, no matter what might be waiting ahead, I know I can endure it because I have you at my side.

To my daughter, Anastasiya: You are my engine of endless inspiration!

To Joy Paolozza, Tatyana Kurilina, Carol Arsenault, Mary Tereshchenko, Ivetta Yaroshenko, Adrienne Gallagher, Anita Day, and Robert Macdonald: You guys are the best. The ultimate best. I thank the universe every day that I am blessed with such loyal, talented, funny, and wonderful friends in my life. Thank you for the endless unconditional love and support.

To Bo and Sophie, the greatest dogs of all time: I love you forever and ever. Let's go buy some treats!

And to all my students, customers, and Instagram followers: There aren't enough words to properly convey the depth of my gratitude. It is such an honor and a pleasure to meet you at shows and classes and to interact with so many of you online. Your pictures, words, and finished projects keep me creating. Thank you for everything!

Olesya Lebedenko

Introduction

This book is a story of three bear friends and their winter craft adventure, full of homemade gifts and cozy memories. They decided to try patchwork, knitting, drawing, and more! So let's take out our fabric scraps, yarn, needles, and scissors and join them.

How to start December? By making fabric boxes with appliquéd designs to hold daily surprises as you count down to the holidays. How to wrap gifts so they stay safe until the holidays? Let our whimsical bears decorate some adorable fabric treat bags. How to make sure that the gifts are opened by the right people? Stitch up some gift tags with knitted hats and pom-poms.

After a snowball fight, get back indoors and thaw out with a mug of your favorite hot drink. Rest your cup on a festive mug rug and keep it warm with a mug cozy embellished with a friendly bear in a knit scarf. Then let your bear friends deliver holiday hugs and winter wishes on quilted patchwork postcards. And the bears have even more surprises in store for you on the pages of this book!

Try any or all of these projects to share holiday joy with your friends and family. And don't forget that you can celebrate the winter holidays at any time of the year!

Stay bright and creative!

Useful Tools and Materials

Here's what you will need to create the projects in this book. I've suggested some of the products that I use, but feel free to use the brands you like best.

- Your amazing fabric scraps (pieces of all sizes and shapes will be perfect for these projects!)
- Embroidery thread for decorative touches
- Paintbrush and embossing stylus (1.2mm or 1.8mm) for characters' face details
- Sewing needles, thread, and pins
- Vellum/tracing paper for templates
- Sharp scissors and pinking shears
- Ruler and rotary cutter
- Postcard rubber stamp and distress ink
- Pencil and water-soluble marker
- Fabric paint in black (or dark brown), white, and red for detail work
- Knitting needles (2.75mm [size US 2]) and cotton yarn in different colors

- Crochet hooks
- Stiletto and eyelets
- Transparent sewing thread (such as Madeira 9763 Monofil #40 in clear)
- Fabric glue (such as Gütermann HT2 Textile Glue)
- Stuffing (such as polyester or cotton)
- Double-sided fusible stabilizer (such as Pellon® 82 Two-Sided Décor Bond®)
- Lightweight double-sided pressure-sensitive fusible web (such as Pellon® Lite EZ-Steam™ II)
- Heavyweight fusible fleece (such as Pellon® 937F)
- Ultra-firm stabilizer (such as Pellon® 70 Peltex® Sew-In Ultra Firm Stabilizer) or polyester interfacing (such as Lazy Girl Designs® Dreamy™ Sew-In Fleece)

Techniques

Before diving into the projects, let's take a few moments to review some basic sewing techniques. I'll start by explaining the steps of making a patchwork block and then move on to the different types of detail work used in the various projects while sharing additional tips and advice.

Constructing the Blocks

All of the patchwork blocks in Part 1 of this book are created with basic techniques. You can easily enlarge them and adapt them for classic paper piecing. I made the blocks with a combination of hand-stitching and machine-stitching. I recommend machine-stitching when the pieces are approximately 1¼" (3cm) or larger, and hand-stitching for the tiny pieces.

To make a patchwork block, transfer the template, cut out all template pieces, and then sew the pieces together following the steps shown in the diagram. The numbers indicate the correct order in which to sew the pieces. If you enlarge the template to adapt it for paper piecing, use the step numbers as the order in which you sew on paper.

Always sew with a ¼" (0.6cm) seam allowance, keeping in mind that the templates **do not** include the seam allowance, and the seam allowance is not pictured in the step-by-step illustrations. Sew the pieces together from edge to edge, unless otherwise noted, and backstitch at both the beginning and end of each seam (if hand-stitching, make knots).

Sewing from Edge to Edge

Sew from edge to edge and press the seam allowance.

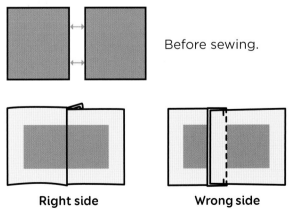

Before sewing.

Right side   **Wrong side**

After sewing from edge to edge.

Cutting the Blocks

All of the block templates are shown at full size: 6" x 6" (15.2 x 15.2cm); you can enlarge or reduce them as desired. Each diagram is printed on a grid with measurements in inches and centimeters. Use these measurements as your starting point when resizing. For best results, use a photocopier to resize the templates.

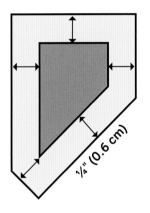

¼" (0.6 cm)

The templates do not include the seam allowance. When cutting your fabric, add a ¼" (0.6cm) seam allowance around each piece.

TIP: To prevent frayed edges and for safety while cutting pieces, I recommend pinking shears.

TIP: If you are machine-stitching your pieces, try a zipper foot for easy seam allowance.

Painting Details

I like fabric paint for adding small details such as facial features (eyes, whiskers, etc.) and decorative elements such as lines and dots. For most of the designs in this book, I use white and black paint. It is essential to use fabric paint if you want your project to be washable. If you need to iron your fabric after painting, be sure to press the wrong side of the fabric or use parchment paper between the fabric and the iron.

To mark the details, first draw them on with either a fine-tipped water-soluble marker or a well-sharpened graphite pencil, then paint over your marks. For eyes and dots, I recommend using an embossing stylus (1.2mm or 1.8mm) or the head of a small pin to apply the paint. To make rosy cheeks, you can use pink water-based pigment ink, a pastel pencil, or chalk (some of these products require ironing to set the color).

Here's a look at the facial details on the Warm Wishes block.

> **TIP:** An advantage of cotton yarn is that you can divide it into strands and use a single strand as sewing thread, so there's no need to search for the exact color or spend extra money on matching thread.

1. Use a very thin brush to fill in the nose and paint the brows over the pencil marks. Use an embossing stylus to make the dots for the eyes.

2. Wait until the paint dries (check the label of your specific product for drying time) and then make a dot on the nose with white paint.

Embellishing with Yarn

I used cotton yarn for the yarn embellishments (knitted features, fringe, and pom-poms) in these projects. You may use whatever type of yarn you wish but be aware that the end results may not look the same as mine if you use something other than cotton yarn.

Knitting

CASTING ON

There is no right or wrong way to cast on (or bind off). Each technique has its own look and characteristics, which may be right for some applications and not suitable for others. In this book, I use a technique that I learned from my grandmother called *long-tail cast on*. You can use any method you're comfortable with, but I encourage you to give my method a try.

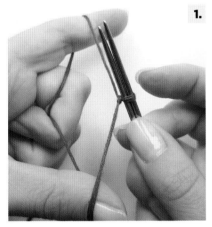

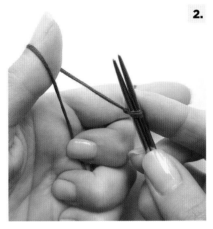

1. Start with a long tail of yarn and make a slipknot over two knitting needles held together. Make sure that the yarn tail is oriented toward you, with the ball of yarn in back. Insert your left thumb and index finger between the two strands of yarn.

2. Holding your left hand like a pistol, close your middle, ring, and pinky fingers around the yarn tail. Insert the needle under the strand that is wrapped around your thumb, then scoop up the strand that is wrapped around your index finger.

3. Bring your yarn out through the thumb loop. Pull your thumb out from the loop of the yarn and pull the yarn to tighten the new stitch.

4. Repeat until you have enough stitches for your project. Make a knot.

5. Pull out one of the knitting needles.

6. Holding the needle with the stitches, knit the first row according to the template.

Basic Stitches

KNIT STITCH

1. Hold the needle with the cast-on stitches in your left hand, with the yarn leading behind your work.
2. Take the other needle in your right hand and insert it into the stitch at the end of the left needle from front to back.
3. Wrap the yarn around in a clockwise fashion. I like to wind the yarn end around my right middle finger once or twice to keep control of it.
4. Pulling the yarn end taut to keep the loop in place, pull the needle back out of the stitch on the left needle.
5. Slide that stitch off the left needle and gently tighten your first stitch.

PURL STITCH

1. Hold the needle with the cast-on stitches in your left hand, with the yarn leading out from the front of your work, then insert the right needle into the next stitch on the left needle from back to front.
2. Wrap the yarn around the right needle in a counterclockwise direction.
3. Slide the tip of the right needle back through the first loop, carrying the new loop with it.
4. Slide the old stitch off the left needle.

GARTER STITCH

Garter stitch, or "knit every row," is one of the easiest and quickest stitch patterns in knitting—the most common way to create garter stitch is by knitting every row. You can also create garter stitch by purling every row.

2 X 2 RIB

1. Row 1: Knit 2 stitches (K2), purl 2 stitches (P2) across the row.
2. Row 2: P2, K2 across the row.
3. Repeat according to template.

FISHERMAN'S RIB

Fisherman's rib makes a fabric with a ribbed appearance but with more depth and softness than standard rib. It is a fun and interesting option for projects such as the postcards and pinkeep.

FISHERMAN'S RIB

1. Purl the first row.

2. On the next row, purl the first stitch.

3. Notice that each knit stitch forms a little "V." You may want to pull your work out just a bit to help you find that "V" the first time. Insert your needle into the center of the "V" in the next knit stitch of the row below.

4. Work a knit stitch just like you normally would, wrapping the working yarn around the needle and pulling it through.

5. Drop the stitch from the left needle. Even though you didn't work that stitch, it's OK to drop it because you've created a new stitch on top of it that's going to extend over two rows.

6. Repeat P1, K1 into the stitch below across the row until you reach the last stitch, then purl the last stitch. As you work across the row, when you come to a knit stitch, you're knitting into the stitch below it; when you come to a purl stitch, you're purling it. This makes it easy to read your knitting without having to remember where you are in the row.

BINDING OFF

For binding off, I use a method called *lace bind off*, shown in the following steps. Try this method or use one that you prefer.

1. K2 together through the back of the loops.

2. Slip the stitch on the right-hand needle to the left-hand needle purlwise.

3. Repeat these steps until there are two stitches left on the left-hand needle.

4. K2 together through the back of the loop. Cut the yarn and pull it through the last stitch.

5. Make a knot through the last stitch to finish.

Decorating with Fringe

1. Cut five 2″ (5.1cm) pieces of yarn. With the hook, pull the loop through the first row.

2. Pull the edges through the loop. Secure by tying a knot. Trim the edges if needed.

Making Pom-Poms

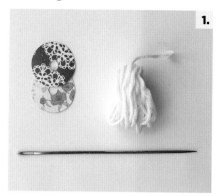

1. Get a piece of cardboard for making templates, yarn, and a long needle. Prepare your templates by cutting out two cardboard circles with a 1″ (2.5cm) diameter, which you will use to make pom-poms for the postcard, candy box, and ornament projects, and two cardboard circles with a 1½″ (3.8cm) diameter, which you will use for the gift tag project. Make a small hole in the middle of each cardboard circle.

2. Make a loop of yarn and put it between two same-sized cardboard rings.

3. With the needle, begin wrapping yarn around the cardboard ring, passing it through the center and the loop of yarn each time. Hold the end of the yarn while you wrap over it to secure it. Work your way around the entire ring, making sure there are no gaps.

4. Cut the end of the yarn, then start snipping through the wrapped yarn all along the edge, positioning your scissors between the two cardboard circles. Be sure to cut through every strand of yarn. Sharp scissors make this task easier.

5. When all the edges are snipped, make a double knot with the loop of yarn that you put between the templates in step 3. Pull the yarn as tight as you can without breaking it.

6. Trim the ends of the loop or leave them long, depending on the project. Remove the cardboard template, fluff the pom-pom, and trim the edges if needed.

Attaching Knitted Elements

To attach knitted details such as scarves, hats, and mittens, use a matching thread to sew them onto the fabric with several stitches.

Tips for Making Stuffed Figures

There are many different kinds of stuffing to choose from when creating stuffed figures. I use a synthetic, medium-weight stuffing that is hypoallergenic and lighter than wool. When choosing stuffing, keep in mind that good-quality stuffing should neither form lumps nor be too smooth. Avoid using layered stuffing. You will find a good selection of stuffing in most quilting and craft shops.

When stuffing a figure, use tweezers and a wooden stick (for example, a chopstick) to get the best results. For small areas, such as the paws and head, shape a piece of stuffing and use tweezers to push it into place. For the body, insert a small amount of stuffing loosely, using the stick to gently move the stuffing to fill the figure without lumps. Add more stuffing until all elements are nice and firm.

Making Decorative Cord from Yarn

Cut a length of yarn (or embroidery floss) at least three the times the desired length of the finished cording (for example, if you need 5" [12.7cm] of cording, cut at least 15" [38.1cm] of yarn or floss). Insert the yarn into your large needle and fold the yarn in half. Tape the doubled-up end of the yarn to the edge of a table. Stand far enough away from the table that the floss is taut but not so tight that it pulls free from the tape. Hold the needle and start twisting the free edge. Twist at least 30 times. Remove the tape. Put the two edges together. Drop the needle. The cording should twist up on itself.

You can help by twisting or straightening the floss as needed until it looks like lovely cording. There could be a few inches at the taped end that don't coil properly. I snip this part off or use to make a knot. Make sure to secure the ends with knots if you don't use the cording right away, otherwise it will untwist at the ends.

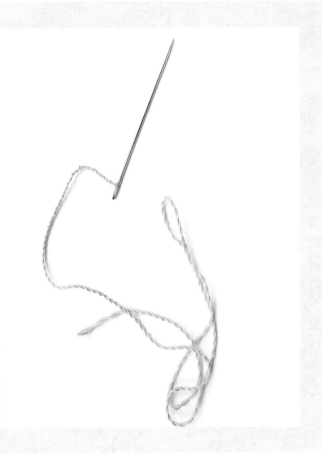

Step-by-Step Block Instructions

For all of the patchwork blocks in Part 1, you will only need small pieces of fabric (less than half of a fat quarter). The block instructions do not include fabric lists; just choose the character you want to make, and try to find everything you need in your treasure trove of fabric scraps.

To help you understand the block-construction diagrams in the projects, here are the step-by-step instructions for creating a block using Warm Wishes (see page 24) as an example. Refer back to these pages for guidance on any of the blocks in Part 1.

1. Choose the fabrics you want to use and gather all needed tools and supplies.

2. Transfer the template onto tracing paper. I mark the fabric with numbers for easier cutting and sewing process; you can use any method you prefer.

3. Trace all template pieces onto the wrong side of the fabric. Cut all pieces with a ¼″ (0.6cm) seam allowance.

> **TIP:** Unless otherwise noted, finish sewing the block before adding any details and decorative touches.

4. Starting with the smallest pieces, pin them (if needed) with the right sides facing each other and sew them together by hand. Press each firmly to get a crisp seam.

5. After you've put the tiny pieces together, you can use a machine for quicker sewing. Pin the pieces and sew from edge to edge.

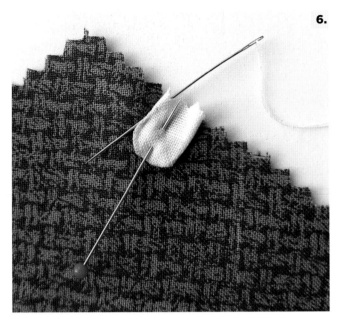

6. Trace the ears with a water-soluble marker on the right side of the fabric. Pin the ears in place. Use the tip of the needle to turn the seam allowance under along the marked line, then blind-stitch.

The finished block with decoration.

7. The block looks like this before any embellishments are added.

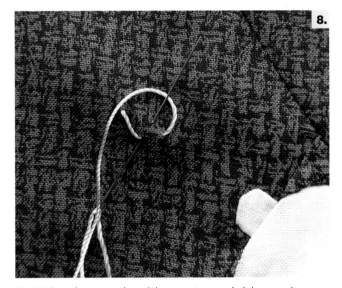

8. Write the words with a water-soluble marker. Divide your embroidery floss into separate strands and use just one strand to stitch the letters in your preferred stitch. Remove the traced lines with a damp cotton swab.

Holly Jolly

Our first character is Brownie, and he is a grizzly bear. He is very excited to share the news that winter has come! It's the first snow of the season, so it's a perfect time for Brownie to wear his fanciest scarf.

6"(15.2cm) QUILT BLOCK &
6" x 4"(15.2 x 10.2cm) POSTCARD
SCALE 1:1

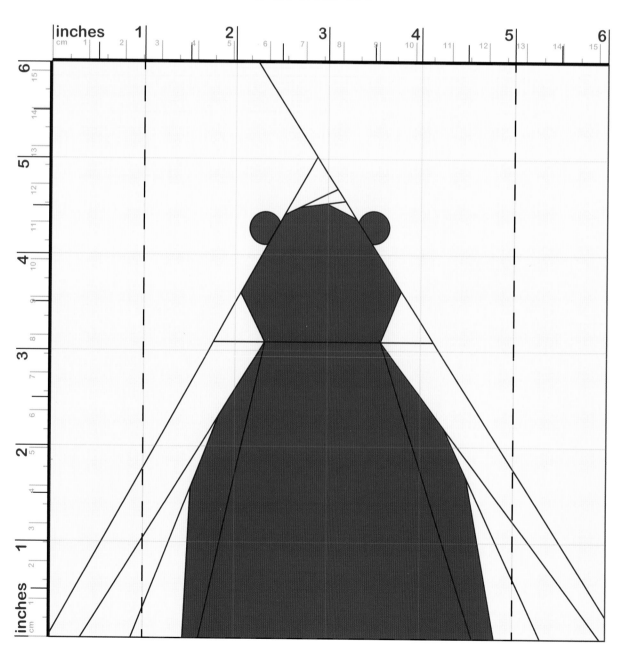

SCARF:

Knit two identical pieces.

Note: Slip first stitch of every row.

Cast on 9 stitches.

Knit 14 rows in loose fisherman's rib (see page 10).

Bind off.

Add fringe (see page 11) to one end of one piece.

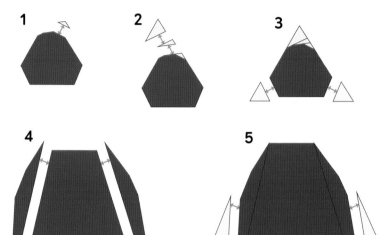

1

2

3

4

5

6

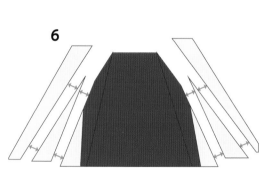

7

8

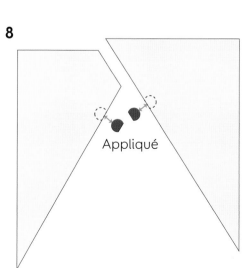

Appliqué

9

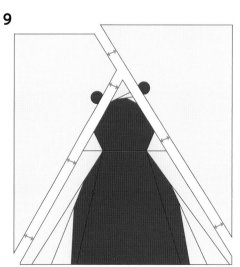

Template on page 72.

Be Bright

Our next character is Honey, the polar bear, dapper in his pom-pom hat and cozy sweater. He wants to celebrate winter's first snow with a cup of something warm, so he made himself a mug of hot cocoa to watch the falling snow.

6"(15.2cm) QUILT BLOCK &
6" x 4"(15.2 x 10.2cm) POSTCARD
SCALE 1:1

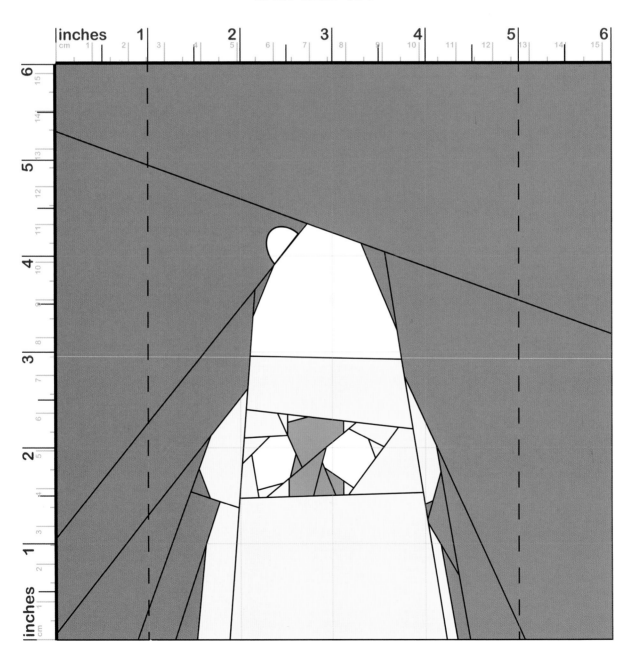

HAT:

Cast on 8 stitches.

Row 1: К3, P2, К3.

Row 2: P3, К2, P3.

Row 3: К2 together, К4, К2 together.

Row 4: Purl.

Row 5: К2 together, К2, К2 together.

Row 6: P2 together, P2 together.

Row 7: К2 together, cut yarn, and pull through last stitch.

Note: See page 12 for instructions on making the pom-pom.

SCARF:

Cast on 16 stitches.

Row 1: Slip 1, К2, P2 three times, К3.

Row 2: Slip 1, P2, К2 three times, P3.

Rows 3-4: Repeat Rows 1-2.

Row 5: Repeat Row 5.

Cast off.

CUFFS:

Knit two identical pieces.

Cast on 6 stitches.

Row 1: К1, P1 three times.

Row 2: P1, К1 three times.

Row 3: Repeat Row 1.

Cast off.

Template on page 73.

Note: Draw the steam with a dry brush and white fabric paint, or you can stitch it with one strand of white embroidery floss if you prefer.

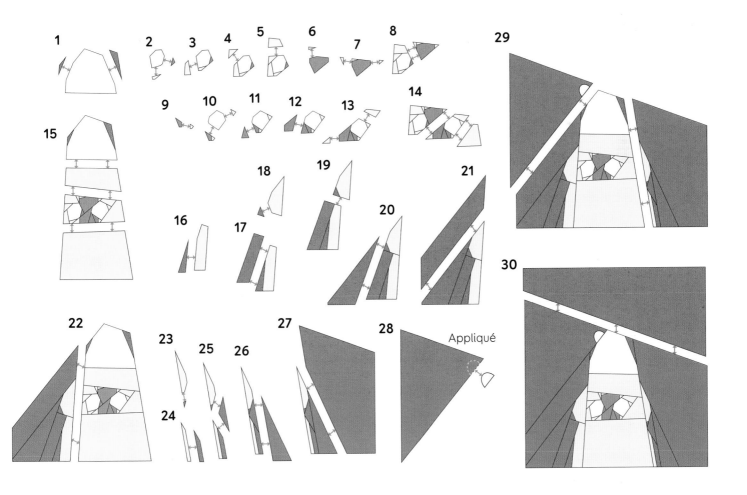

Joyful Wishes

Our third bear friend is a panda named Whimsy. He is always in a rush and, like all pandas, is cute and clumsy. With winter holidays approaching, he's decided that it's the perfect time for a present wrapped up with a cheery red bow.

6"(15.2cm) QUILT BLOCK &
6" x 4"(15.2 x 10.2cm) POSTCARD
SCALE 1:1

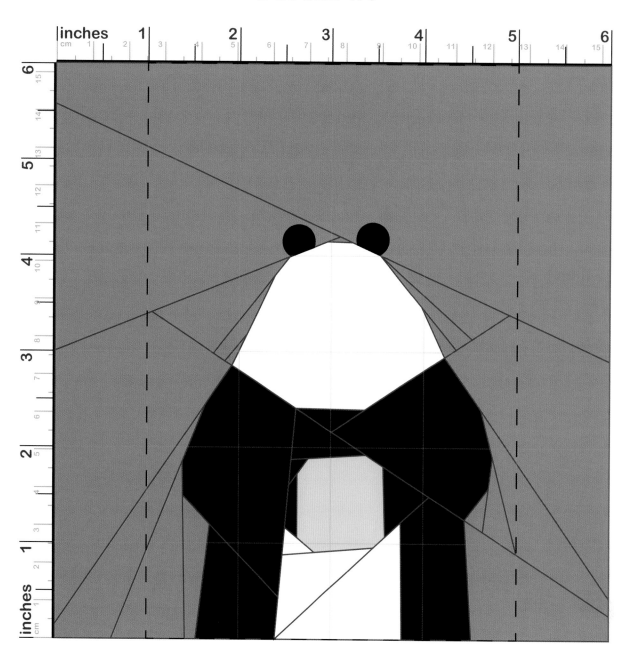

LEFT MITTEN:

Cast on 7 stitches.

Knit 5 rows in K1, P1 rib.

Row 6: Knit to last stitch, knit into front and back of stitch (1 stitch increase).

Row 7: Purl into front and back of first stitch, purl to end of row.

Row 8: Knit to last 2 stitches, K2 together.

Row 9: P2 together, purl to end of row.

Row 10: K2 together, knit to last 2 stitches, K2 together.

Row 11: P2 together, purl to last 2 stitches, P2 together.

Row 12: K3 together, cut yarn, pull end through last stitch on needle.

RIGHT MITTEN:

Cast on 7 stitches.

Knit 5 rows in K1, P1 rib.

Row 6: Knit into front and back of first stitch, knit to end of row.

Row 7: Purl to last stitch, purl into front and back of last stitch.

Row 8: K2 together, knit to end of row.

Row 9: Purl to last 2 stitches, P2 together.

Row 10: K2 together, knit to last 2 stitches, K2 together.

Row 11: P2 together, purl to last 2 stitches, P2 together.

Row 12: K3 together, cut yarn, pull end through last stitch on needle.

Template on page 74.

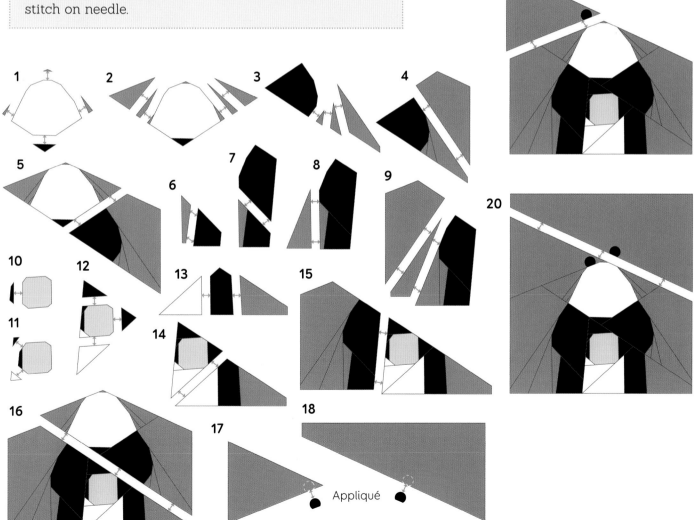

Toasty Hugs

Brownie made a present for one of his friends! To keep warm while delivering the gift, he wrapped himself up in his extra-long, extra-thick scarf. To make the bow on the present, I used a piece of thin string.

6"(15.2cm) QUILT BLOCK &
6" x 4"(15.2 x 10.2cm) POSTCARD
SCALE 1:1

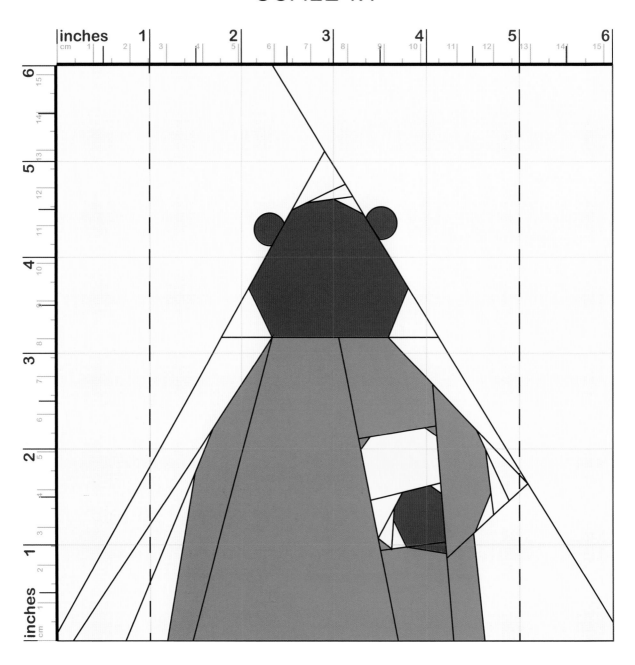

LEFT SIDE OF SCARF (LOOP):

Note: Slip first stitch of every row.

Cast on 7 stitches.

Knit 28 rows in garter stitch (see page 10).

Cast off.

RIGHT SIDE OF SCARF:

Cast on 7 stitches.

Knit 4 rows in K1, P1.

Knit 46 rows in garter stitch.

Knit 4 rows in K1, P1 1 rib.

Cast off.

To loop the scarf after knitting, fold both pieces in half. Attach the loop to the left side with the edges inside. Attach the second piece with stitches in the middle, then pull the ends through the loop.

CUFF:

Cast on 7 stitches.

Knit 4 rows in K1, P1 rib.

Cast off.

Gather cast-on stitches when attaching the cuff to the fabric.

Template on page 75.

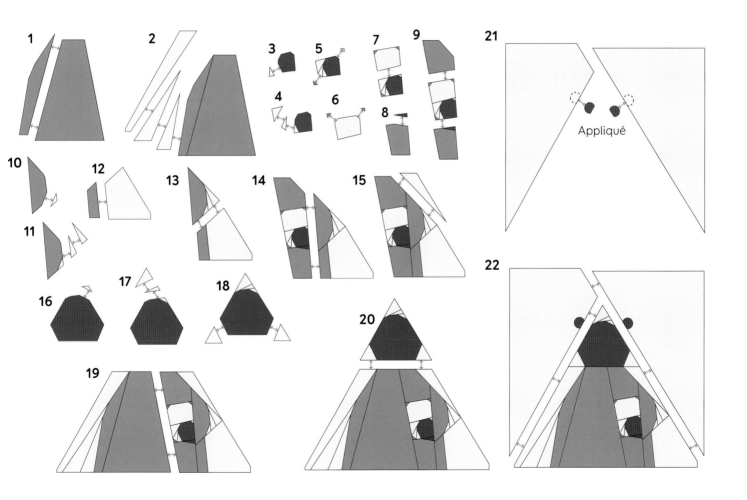

Warm Wishes

Inside Brownie's gift box was this lovely, fluffy scarf that he made for Honey. The block is an easy, quick project. Try multicolored yarn to make the scarf really stand out!

6"(15.2cm) QUILT BLOCK &
6" x 4"(15.2 x 10.2cm) POSTCARD
SCALE 1:1

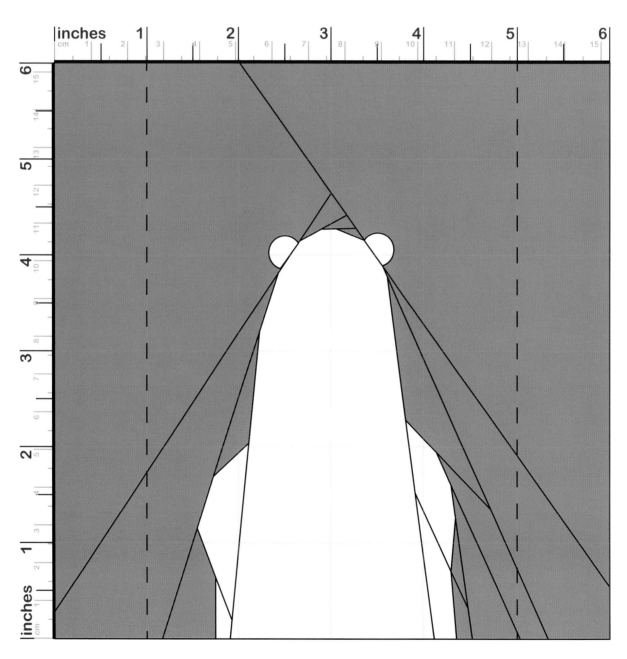

SCARF:

Slip first stitch of every row.

Knit two identical pieces.

Cast on 9 stitches.

Knit 14 rows in loose fisherman's rib (see page 10).

Cast off.

Add fringe (see page 11) to one end of one piece.

Attach the non-fringed piece horizontally, then attach the fringed piece vertically over the middle of the first piece.

Template on page 76.

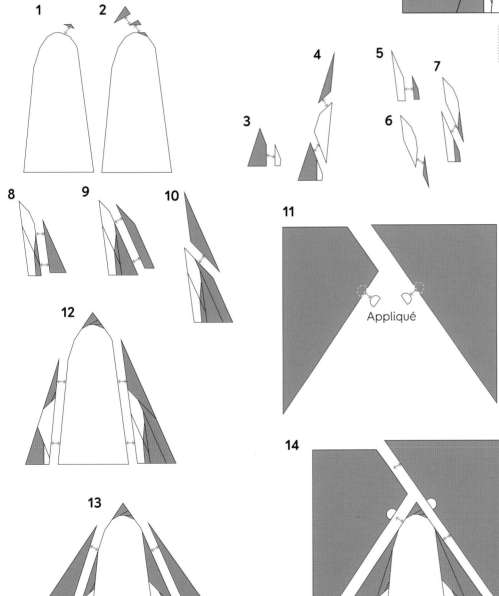

1

2

3

4

5

6

7

8

9

10

11

Appliqué

12

13

14

Stay Cozy

Whimsy decided to surprise his friends with his new accessories. He had so much fun knitting the hat that he went on to make a shawl with fringe. Look how cute he is! Whimsy is certainly a creative panda.

6"(15.2cm) QUILT BLOCK &
6" x 4"(15.2 x 10.2cm) POSTCARD
SCALE 1:1

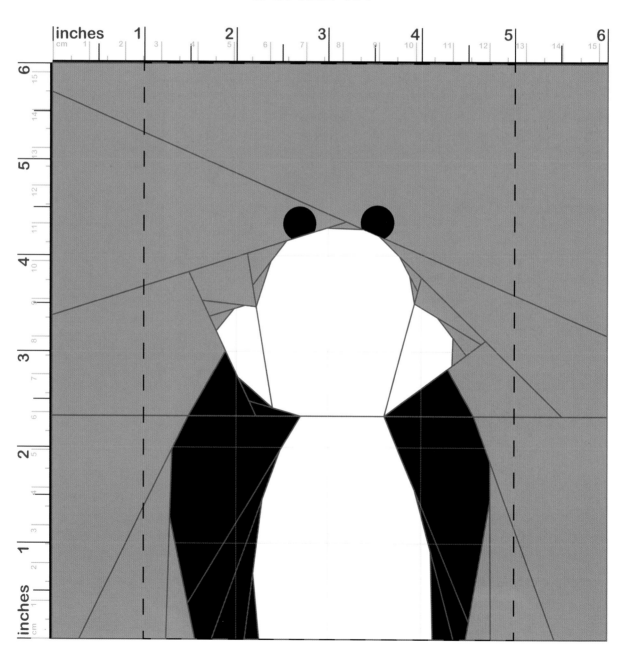

HAT:

Cast on 14 stitches.

Row 1: Knit.

Row 2: K2 together, knit to last 2 stitches. K2 together.

Rows 3–6: Repeat row 2.

Row 7: Cast off.

Pick up and K4 at beginning of cast-on edge.

Knit 4 rows in garter stitch (see page 10).

Cast off, leaving a small tail.

Tie a small piece of yarn at bottom of tail.

Repeat at other end of cast-on row.

To decorate the hat, use a sewing needle to make a running stitch in another color.

TOP (FRINGED) PIECE OF SHAWL:

Cast on 18 stitches.

Row 1: Slip 1, knit to last 2 stitches, K2 together.

Row 2: K2 together, knit to end of row.

Rows 3–16: Repeat rows 1 and 2 until 2 stitches remain.

Row 17: K2 together.

Cut yarn, leaving a 2" (5cm) tail, put through last stitch.

Add fringe (see page 11) to shaped edge.

NECK PIECE OF SHAWL:

Cast on 30 stitches.

Knit 11 rows in garter stitch.

Cast off.

Template on page 77.

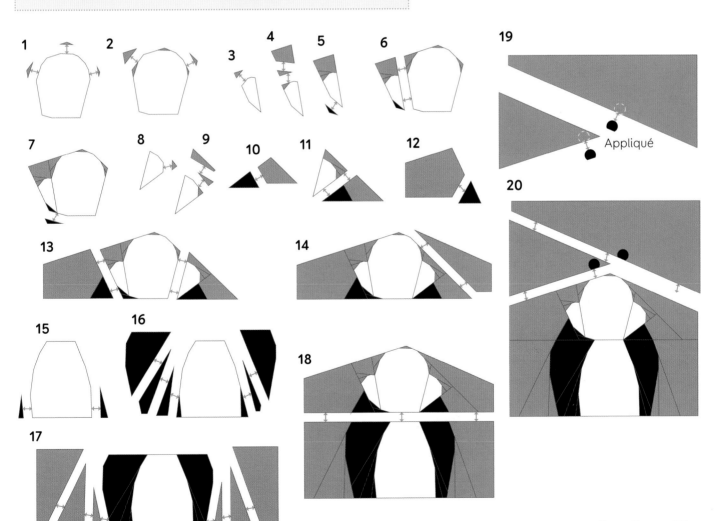

Postcard

Since the first postcards were created and mailed in the mid-1800s, the practice of sending and collecting warm memories on postcards blossomed and still is popular today. Postcards have always meant a lot to me, as both of my grandfathers were military officers, and they moved so often that it was hard to keep track of how many towns they had lived in. To keep in touch, they would send postcards with creative designs and colorful images. People still love postcards, whether to send to family and friends or to keep as mementos of special places visited.

What if you created your own postcards and took it up a notch by decorating your messages with fabrics and stitches? Here, I'll show you how to make adorable 3D postcards with the patchwork blocks from the previous section—our winter bear friends will deliver your warm thoughts with care!

YOU WILL NEED:

- Patchwork bear block of choice, trimmed to postcard size (4" x 6" [10.2 x 15.2cm])
- Knitted embellishments for bear block (not yet attached)
- 22" x 1¼" (55.9 x 3.2cm) bias tape for binding (optional)
- One piece backing fabric, 4" x 6" (10.2 x 15.2cm)
- Sewing needles, thread, and pins
- Pencil or water-soluble marker
- Fabric paint, black (or dark brown)
- Embossing stylus (1.2mm or 1.8mm) and thin paintbrush
- Scissors with sharp tips and pinking shears
- Two pieces two-sided fusible stabilizer, 4" x 6" (10.2 x 15.2cm) each
- One piece ultra-firm stabilizer, 4" x 6" (10.2 x 15.2cm) each
- Distress inks and postcard stamp (or micropigment ink pen if you prefer to draw the back of the postcard)

Note: The following instructions show you how to attach binding, but you can leave raw edges if you prefer.

1. Stamp or draw the postcard features on the backing fabric. Make a sandwich: ultra-firm stabilizer (polyester interfacing piece), then two-sided fusible stabilizer, then backing. Press together with steam.

2. Add to the sandwich. On the wrong side of the patchwork block, place the second piece of two-sided fusible stabilizer and then the pressed backing/stabilizer piece. Press with steam.

4. Pin the bias tape. Start stitching with a ¼" (0.6cm) seam allowance, leaving 1½" (3.8cm) from the edge of the bias. As you approach a corner, lay the binding along the edge up to the corner, then, using a ruler, mark a line ¼" (0.6cm) in and up from the corner (I do not do this in advance in case the fabric shifts).

3. Trim the sandwich.

5. Secure your stitch with several stitches. Flip your binding straight up over the edge, pressing with your fingers to create a bias corner. Flip the binding back over itself, making sure to keep the bias crease you created in place. When you line the binding back up, it should line up perfectly with the edge of the bias crease you created and the raw edge of the postcard. Pin if needed. Bring it back under the presser foot and stitch ¼" (0.6cm) away from the edge; be sure to backstitch at the beginning to secure the bias in place. Repeat these steps for all corners.

6. Similar to how you started the binding, leave 1½" (3.8cm) loose binding to be able to join the two ends. For small projects, like postcards, make a cardboard template for diagonal lines. Leave ¼" (0.6cm) and draw a line. Cut the extra bias.

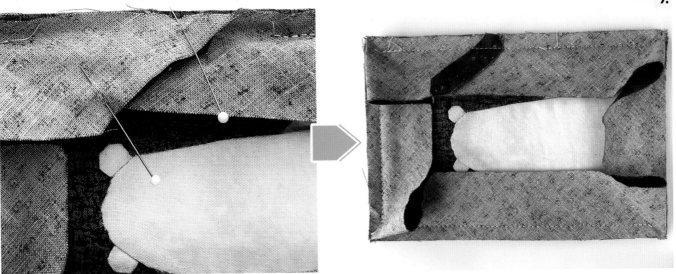

7. Pin and stitch directly on the marked line, joining the two ends. Trim the corners. Press the seam open. Stitch to finish.

8. Press back the binding.

9. Fold the bias twice and press. Form the corners and clip.

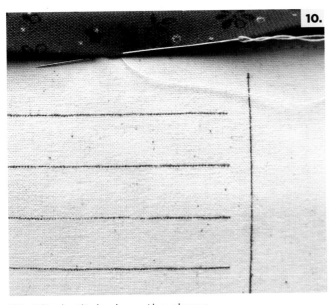

10. Blind-stitch along the shape.

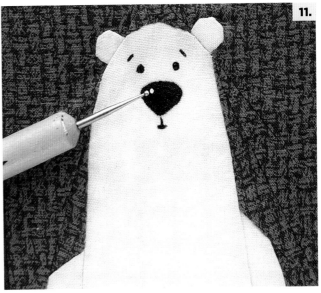

11. Attach the knitted embellishments and create the face details (see page 8).

Pinkeep

I love making winter-themed decorations. I use these fun pinkeeps as door décor for each room in the house during Christmastime. This project also makes a great last-minute holiday gift. Make a pinkeep using one of our bear friends from the previous section.

YOU WILL NEED:

- Patchwork bear block of choice, 6" x 6" (15.2 x 15.2cm)
- Knitted embellishments for bear block (not yet attached)
- Two pieces cardboard, 5½" x 5½" (14 x 14cm) each
- One piece backing fabric, 7½" x 7½" (19.1 x 19.1cm)

- Sewing needles, thread, and pins
- Scissors with sharp tips and pinking shears
- Fabric paint, black (or dark brown) and white
- Embossing stylus (1.2mm or 1.8mm) and thin paintbrush

- Transparent sewing thread
- Fabric glue
- Two pieces one-sided fusible fleece, 7½" x 7½" (19.1 x 19.1cm) each
- Ruler and rotary cutter

1. Make two sandwiches: one with the patchwork block and a piece of one-sided fusible fleece; the other with the backing piece and a piece of one-sided fusible fleece. Press both with steam.

2. Attach all knitted decorations, create the bear's face details, and stitch the lettering (see pages 8, 12, 15).

3. Make a running stitch across the top of the block until you reach the corner. Place a piece of cardboard on the wrong side of the block.

Back of pinkeep.

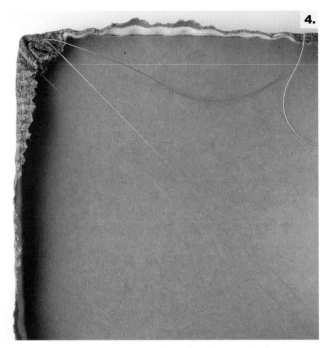

4. Slightly pull the thread. Make long stitches to the next corner and pull.

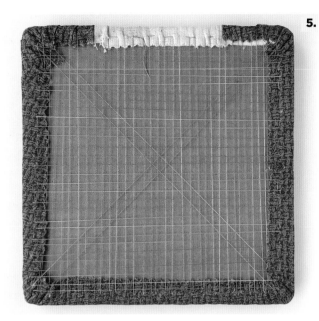

5. Repeat this process from corner to corner so that the entire border of the block is fixed and tight to the cardboard.

6. Repeat steps 3–5 with the backing piece.

8. Use transparent sewing thread to sew the cord with whipstitch along the edge of the square.

> **TIP:** Instead of transparent thread, you can use a thread that is the same color as the cord.

7. Cut 18″ (45.7cm) of cord (see page 13). Make knots on both ends and make a loop. Affix each end between the front piece and the backing piece. To decorate around the edge of the square, prepare approximately 25½″ (64.8cm) of cord. Make a knot on both ends. Put one end of the cord between the front and back sides of the project. Pin both sides together and stitch around the square with a strong thread that will not break as you pull it to attach the two sides.

9. With a stiletto, push the second end of the cord between the front and back sides. Make several stitches to secure.

Framed Present

Curious bears having fun in wooden frames make great decorations to hang on the wall during the winter holidays—or even throughout the entire winter! Even better, make a few of these framed fabric pictures to give as holiday gifts. They will be a welcome part of the winter festivities year after year.

YOU WILL NEED:

- Patchwork bear block of choice, 6" x 6" (15.2 x 15.2cm)
- Knitted embellishments for bear block (not yet attached)
- One piece cardboard, 5½" x 5½" (14 x 14cm)
- One piece scrapbooking paper for backing, 5½" x 5½" (14 x 14cm)
- Sewing needles, thread, and pins
- Scissors with sharp tips and pinking shears
- Fabric paint, black (or dark brown) and white
- Embossing stylus (1.2mm or 1.8mm) and thin paintbrush
- Fabric glue
- One piece one-sided fusible fleece, 7½" x 7½" (19.1 x 19.1cm)
- Wooden frame, 6" x 6" (15.2 x 15.2cm) (For this project, I used a custom, hand-painted frame by Mill Hill®.)
- Ruler and rotary cutter
- Clips

1. Make a sandwich with the patchwork bear block and one-sided fusible fleece. Press. Attach all knitted embellishments, create the facial details, and stitch the lettering on the bear block.

2. Attach the block to the piece of cardboard (see steps 3–5 of Pinkeep, page 34).

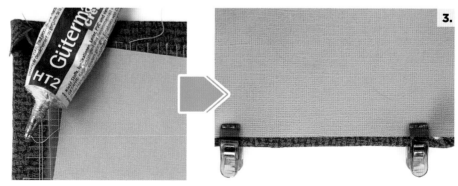

3. Glue on the backing and clip it until the glue dries. Frame the block once the glue is dry.

Treat Bag

If your stockings are not enough for all your Christmas treats, make some of these festive treat bags! These handmade bags adorned with charming characters are presents in their own right.

YOU WILL NEED:

- Patchwork bear block of choice (Stay Cozy is pictured in the project steps)
- Knitted embellishments for bear block (not yet attached)
- One fabric strip, 2¼" x 9¾" (5.7 x 24.8cm)

- Two fabric strips, 2" x 6½" (5.1 x 16.5cm) each
- Two fabric strips, 4½" x 9¾" (11.4 x 24.8cm) each
- One piece backing fabric, 8½" x 9¾" (21.6 x 24.8cm)
- Two pieces lining fabric, 9¾" x 12½" (24.8 x 31.8cm) each

- Sewing needles, thread, and pins
- Fabric paint, black (or dark brown) and white
- Embossing stylus (1.2mm or 1.8mm) and thin paintbrush
- Ruler and rotary cutter

1. Put the 2″ x 6½″ (5.1 x 16.5cm) fabric strips on the right and left sides of the bear block, right sides together. Pin and stitch together with a ¼″ (0.6cm) seam allowance. Put the 2¼″ x 9¾″ (5.7 x 24.8cm) fabric strip at the bottom of the block, right sides together; pin and stitch. Put one of the 4½″ x 9¾″ (11.4 x 24.8cm) strips at the top of the block, right sides together; pin and stitch. Press down firmly. Stitch the backing fabric and the other 4½″ x 9¾″ (11.4 x 24.8cm) strip. Press down firmly.

2. Put one piece of lining and the backing with the right sides together; pin and stitch. Repeat with the other piece of lining and the front of the bag. Press the seams.

3. Attach the knitted embellishments to the bear block, create the facial details, and stitch the lettering (see pages 8, 12, 15).

4. To make a casing for the drawstring, measure down 1½″ (3.8cm) from the seam and mark. Then measure ½″ (1.3cm) from the first mark and mark again.

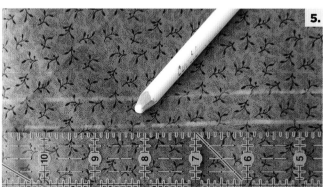

5. Pin with right sides together. Stitch all the way around, leaving a gap between the two marked lines on both sides. Make sure that seams match. Leave a gap of least 3″ (7.6cm) on the bottom of the lining for turning right sides out. Turn right sides out and press. Mark lines 1½″ (3.8cm) and 2″ (5.1cm) from the top edge with pastel pencil or chalk. Stitch all the way around on the drawn lines.

6. Cut two 24″ (61cm) lengths of cord (see page 13). Attach a safety pin to one end of the cord and run it all the way through the casing. Repeat on the other side. Knot the ends of the cord.

Mug Cozy

This happy bear motif cheers up a simple cozy, sized to fit an individual coffee mug or teacup and keep your hot drink warm and delicious. You can easily enlarge the template to fit over a teapot. I created this project specially for my tea-loving friends Bob and Anita.

YOU WILL NEED:

- Patchwork bear block of choice, 6" x 6" (15.2 x 15.2cm)
- Knitted embellishments for bear block (not yet attached)
- Two pieces lining fabric, 10½" x 8½" (26.7 x 21.6cm) each
- Two pieces one-sided fusible fleece, 10½" x 8½" (26.7 x 21.6cm) each
- Two pieces backing fabric, 8½" x 9¾" (21.6 x 24.8cm) each
- One fabric strip for loop, 1" x 3" (2.5 x 7.6cm)
- Bias strips for binding, 1⅜" x 22" (3.5 x 55.9cm) and 1⅜" x 24" (3.5 x 61cm)
- Fabric paint, black (or dark brown) and white
- Embossing stylus (1.2mm or 1.8mm) and thin paintbrush
- Sewing needles, thread, and pins
- Sharp scissors and pinking shears

1. Trace the mug cozy template and cut out the lining, backing, and one-sided fusible fleece.

2. Cut pieces with ¼" (0.6cm) seam allowance for the front piece. Pin and sew the pieces together; trim edges to the template if needed.

3. Iron the fusible fleece to the wrong side of the backing and front motif piece.

4. Attach the knitted embellishments, create the face details, and stitch the lettering. Make two sandwiches with the lining and ironed pieces, wrong sides together, then hand- or machine-quilt each of them (see pages 8, 12, 15).

Template
on page 82.

5.

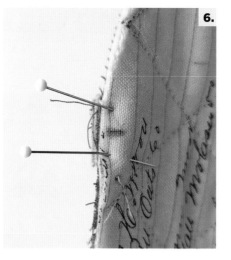

6.

8.

5. Make a loop with the 1″ x 3″ (2.5 x 7.6cm) fabric strip. Press under ¼″ (0.6cm) to the wrong side along each of the long sides, then fold the strip in half and press.

6. Matching the edges of the folds, sew along the long side. Fold the backing piece in half and mark the middle. Fold the loop in half. Pin the face to the right side of the backing piece. Put the backing and front pieces together, lining sides in, and pin along the curved edge.

7. Pin and stitch along the edge of the 1⅜″ x 24″ (3.5 x 61cm) bias strip. Cut extra bias if needed. Press and blind-stitch the bias.

8. Make several stitches to secure the loop to the binding.

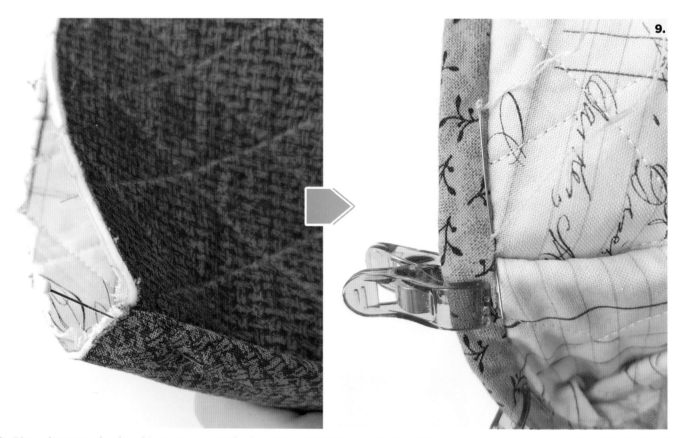

9.

9. Pin edges to the backing piece. With the 1⅜″ x 22″ (3.5 x 55.9cm) bias strip, press, sew with a ¼″ (0.6cm) seam allowance, then blind-stitch along the edge in the same manner as step 7.

Gift Tags

A pretty gift tag is a perfect finishing touch for a beautifully wrapped present. When you add a special message to the tag, it's almost like sending a smile or a warm hug. I will show you how to make two different types of gift tags: one with curved edges and knitted decorations, and one with raw-edge appliqué.

Tag with Knitted Pom-Pom Hat

YOU WILL NEED:

- Pencil or water-soluble marker
- Knitting needles (2.75mm [size US 2]) and cotton yarn
- Stiletto and eyelets
- Two-sided fusible stabilizer
- Sewing needles, thread, and pins
- Fabric in two different colors
- Parchment paper
- Sharp scissors and pinking shears
- Pigment ink pen
- One piece decorative cording for loop

HAT:

Cast on 16 stitches

Row 1: K3, P2, (K2, P2) twice, K3.

Row 2: P3, K2, (P2, K2) twice, P3.

Repeat rows 1 and 2 once each and row 1 once more.

Row 6: K2 together, knit across row until last 2 stitches, K2 together.

Repeat row 6 until two stitches left.

Last row: K2 together.

Cut yarn and pull through the loop.

Add pom-pom (see page 12).

These templates plus three additional designs on pages 78–80.

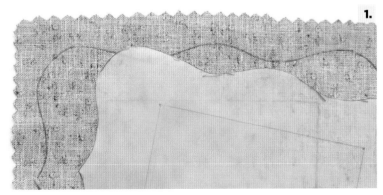

1. Trace the tag template onto the wrong side of the fabric.

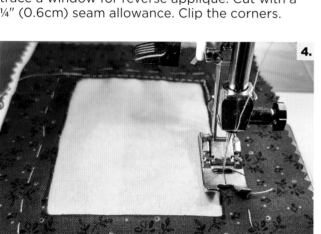

2. With your pencil or water-soluble marker, trace a window for reverse appliqué. Cut with a ¼″ (0.6cm) seam allowance. Clip the corners.

3. Pin and make a running stitch around the window, following the shape.

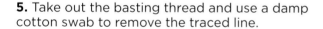

4. Remember to leave ¼″ (0.6cm) seam allowance. Stitch along the edge of the window.

5. Take out the basting thread and use a damp cotton swab to remove the traced line.

6. Transfer the template onto one side of the stabilizer. Iron through the parchment to the wrong side of the fabric with the window in the middle.

7. Fold the fabric right sides together. Pin and stitch, following the shape of the curved edge.

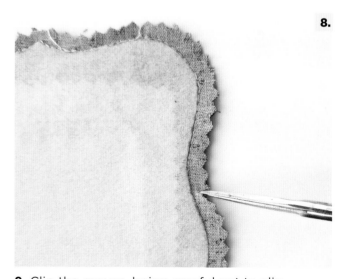

8. Clip the curves, being careful not to clip the stitches.

9. Pull up the backing fabric and cut to turn the piece right sides out.

11. Use scissors to enlarge the hole for the eyelet if needed. Insert the eyelet shaft through the hole.

12. Use a hammer or similar tool with some force to crush the shaft of the eyelet over the fabric.

14. Create the hat and pom-pom according to the template, then attach it to the gift tag (see page 12).

TIP: There are several ways of putting eyelets in fabric. I used scrapbooking eyelets that are thinner and easier to work with on tiny projects.

10. Use a stiletto to make a hole.

13. Write "From" and "To" on the tag with pigment ink.

15. Attach a loop of cord through the eyelet (see page 13).

Three Presents Tag with Raw-Edge Appliqué

1. Trace the tag template onto the right side of the fabric with a water-soluble marker.

2. Put fabric scraps on the stabilizer and press through parchment paper.

3. Transfer the decoration templates onto the right side of your fabric scraps, then cut them out without a seam allowance.

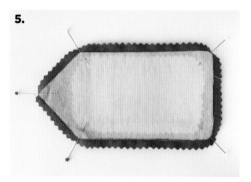

4. Cut a piece of yarn and place it down the middle of the right side of the fabric. Arrange the decorations and press, then sew each element in place by stitching around the edges of the shapes.

5. Pin the front and the backing piece with right sides together. Sew around the shape, leaving the bottom (in this photo, the left side) open.

6. Turn right sides out and press. Blind-stitch the opening.

7. Follow steps 10–15 on page 43 to insert the eyelet and attach the cord loop.

YOU WILL NEED:

- Pencil or water-soluble marker
- Stiletto and eyelets
- Two-sided fusible stabilizer
- Sewing needles, thread, and pins
- Fabric in two different colors
- Parchment paper
- Sharp scissors and pinking shears
- Pigment ink pen
- 9"–10" (25–30cm) long piece decorative cording for loop

Stuffed Ornament

Our three bear friends are ready for winter, all bundled up in their beautiful knitted scarves. You could hang them on your tree, give them as holiday gifts, or add them to a decorative display where they can listen to your family's stories.

YOU WILL NEED:

- Pencil or water-soluble marker
- Knitting needles (2.75mm [size US 2])
- Cotton yarn for the scarf and loop
- Black and white fabric for panda, brown fabric for brown bear, or white fabric for polar bear
- Piece of cardboard, 1" x 1" (2.5 x 2.5cm)
- Sewing needles, thread, and pins
- Stuffing, wooden stick, and tweezers
- Embossing stylus (1.2mm or 1.8mm) and thin paintbrush
- Fabric paint, black (or dark brown), white, and red
- Sharp scissors and pinking shears
- Small decorative items for bear to hold

SCARF: (knitted elements for all three figures are the same)

Note: Slip first stitch of every row.

Cast on 7 stitches.

Knit 45 rows in loose fisherman's rib (see page 10).

Cast off.

Add fringe or pom-poms to both ends of the scarf (see pages 11–12).

Templates on page 81.

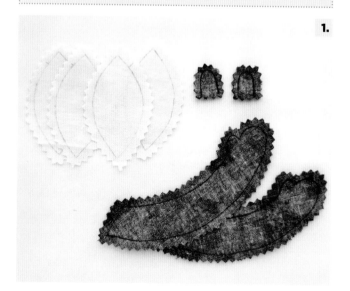

1. Trace the head template four times on the wrong side of the template. Cut with a ¼" (0.6cm) seam allowance. Fold the fabric twice with right sides together. Trace the ear template twice. Pin and sew along the shape, leaving the bottom open. Cut with a ¼" (0.6cm) seam allowance.

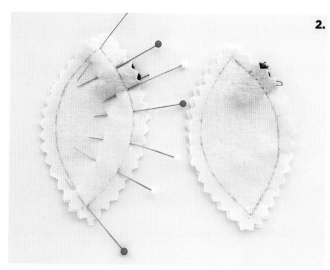

2. Pin one ear between two parts of the head. Sew along the edge. Repeat for second ear.

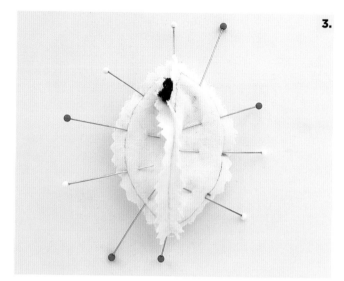

3. Pin the sewn part of the head. Sew along the shape, leaving a ½" (1.3cm) opening.

4. Trace the paw template twice on the wrong side of the fabric. Sew along the shape, leaving openings at the bottom. Cut with a ¼" (0.6cm) seam allowance. Turn right sides out and press. Turn the head right sides out.

5. Stuff the head and paws gently with tweezers and blind-stitch the openings.

6. If making the panda, trace and cut the eye spots with a ¼" (0.6cm) seam allowance. With a stiletto, press the seam allowance to the wrong side of the fabric.

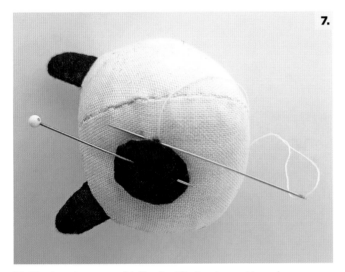

7. Pin in place and blind-stitch along the shape.

8. Create the face details and make a tongue with several stitches. Add the pupils and the white dot on the nose.

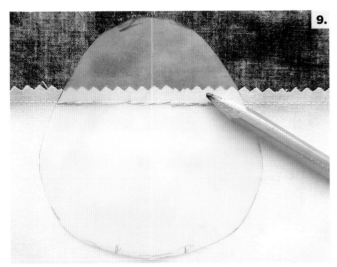

9. Trace the body template. (For the panda's body, stitch the black and white fabrics together. Press the seam allowance to the top.)

10. Fold the fabric with right sides together, matching the line of stitches. Pin and stitch along the shape, leaving an opening at the bottom for stuffing.

11. Turn right sides out. Gently stuff the body.

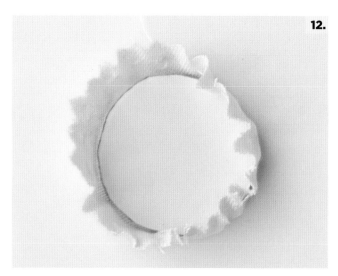

12. Trace the circular template onto the cardboard and cut out. Cut a circle of white fabric with a 1½″ (3.8cm) diameter. Make a running stitch, place the cardboard circle in the middle of the fabric circle, and gently pull the thread. Make several stitches to secure.

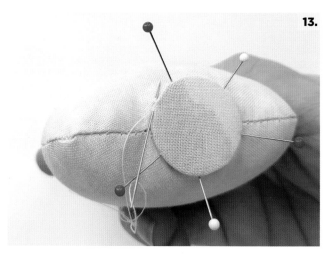

13. Pin the covered cardboard circle to the bottom of the body to hide the opening. Blind-stitch to secure.

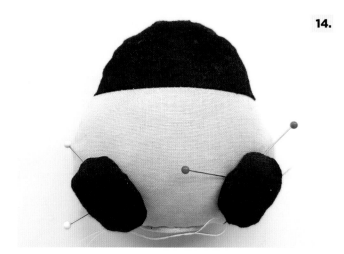

14. Pin the back paws (feet) in place and blind-stitch to secure. Repeat for the front paws (arms and hands). Attach the two front paws together with several stitches.

15. Pin and attach the head with blind stitching.

16. With a dry paintbrush, add the details to the paws.

17. Cut 9″ (22.9cm) of cord (see page 13). Make a loop and attach it to the top of the head with several stitches.

18. Make a bouquet with a tiny apple or orange and a cinnamon stick. Wrap the scarf around the bear's neck and place the bouquet in his arms.

Back view of brown bear.

Candy Cone

Our bears have a bounty of treats to share! When I was a child, when you bought candies or nuts, they would come wrapped in paper cones. I can still remember the smell of the paper mixed with the sweet aroma of the treats. During the holidays, you can fill these fabric cones with goodies and give them as gifts or display them as decorations.

YOU WILL NEED:

- Black and white fabric for panda, brown fabric for brown bear, or white fabric for polar bear
- Fabric for outside of cone, 9" x 10" (22.7 x 25.4cm)
- Lining fabric, 9" x 10" (22.7 x 25.4cm)
- Cord or lace, 17" (43.2cm) long
- Fabric paint, black (or dark brown) and white
- Embossing stylus (1.2 mm or 1.8mm) and thin paintbrush
- Pastel pencil
- Sewing needles, thread, and pins
- Sharp scissors and pinking shears
- Stuffing and tweezers
- One piece one-sided fusible fleece, 8" x 10" (20.3 x 25.4cm)
- One piece two-sided fusible stabilizer, 8" x 10" (20.3 x 25.4cm)

1. Transfer the template onto the wrong side of the outer fabric and the lining. Cut each with a ¼" (0.6cm) seam allowance. Transfer the template onto the fleece and stabilizer. Cut each with no seam. Pin the front piece and the lining with right sides together and sew along the curved edge on the top of the cone.

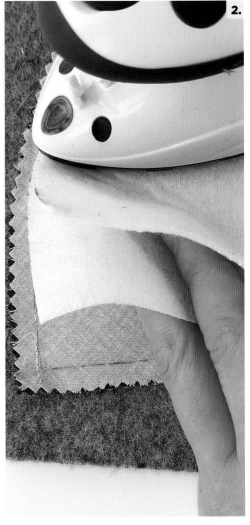

2. Place a piece of stabilizer and fusible fleece on the wrong side of the front fabric. Press with steam.

3. Unfold the cone so that the seam is across the middle, then fold it right sides together the opposite way. Pin and sew along the line, leaving a 3" (7.6cm) opening in the lining. Turn right sides out.

Templates on pages 81–82.

4. Make a loop of out of the cord (see page 13) or lace. Knot one edge. With a long needle, pull the cord through the side.

5. Sew through the opposite side. Remove the needle and make a knot at the second edge to secure the cord.

6. Sew the opening with blind stitches. Push the lining into the stabilized part. Iron the cone with steam.

7.

9.

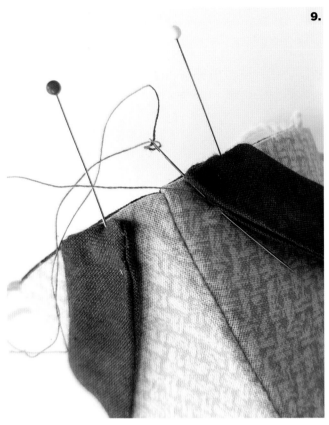

7. Fold the bear fabric with right sides together. Transfer the template for the paws and ears. Pin and sew along the shapes, leaving openings at the bottom. Cut with a ¼" (0.6cm) seam allowance. On each paw, clip the curve where the thumb meets the rest of the paw. Turn right sides out and press.

8. Make the head, referring to steps 1–5 of the Stuffed Ornament project (see pages 46–47).

9. Insert the seam allowance at the top of the paws. Position and pin the paws as if they're wrapped around the cone, holding it. Blind-stitch along the shape.

10.

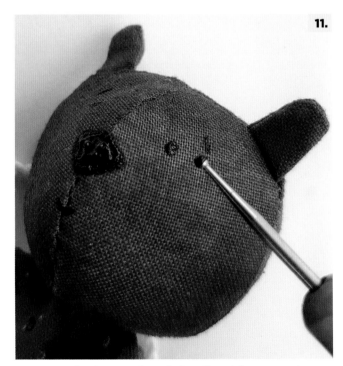

11.

10. Pin the head and secure it with several blind stitches.

11. Draw the bear's facial details with a pastel pencil and then paint over them with fabric paint.

Cookie Bowl

You know that Christmas is just around the corner when you smell the unforgettable aroma of gingerbread cookies baking! Fill these bowls with cookies for a holiday display that is as delicious as it is decorative.

YOU WILL NEED:

- Black and white fabric for panda, brown fabric for brown bear, or white fabric for polar bear
- Fabric for sides of bowl, 3¼" x 21" (8.25 x 53cm)
- Fabric for bottom of bowl, 6" x 6" (15.25 x 15.25cm)
- Lining fabric for sides and bottom of bowl
- Three bias strips for binding, 1½" x 21" (3.8 x 53.3cm) each
- Cord or lace, 17" (43.2cm) long
- Fabric paint, black (or dark brown) and white
- Embossing stylus (1.2mm or 1.8mm) and thin paintbrush
- Pastel pencil
- Sewing needles, thread, and pins
- Sharp scissors and pinking shears
- Knitting needles (2.75mm [size US 2]) and several colors of cotton yarn
- Stuffing and tweezers
- Ultra-firm stabilizer for sides and bottom of bowl
- One-sided fusible fleece for sides of bowl
- Two pieces ultra-firm stabilizer for bottom of bowl

Templates on page 82.

SCARF:

Note: Slip first stitch of every row.

Cast on 7 stitches.

Knit 54 rows in loose fisherman's rib (see page 10).

Cast off.

Add fringe or pom-poms to both ends of the scarf (see pages 11-12).

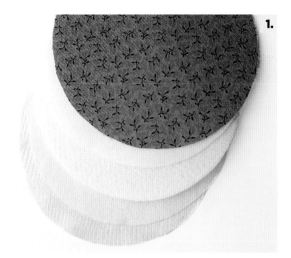

1. Trace a 6″ (15.25cm) diameter circle onto and cut the following: one piece of bowl fabric, one piece of lining fabric, two pieces of two-sided fusible stabilizer, and one piece of ultra-firm stabilizer.

2. Make a sandwich to form the bottom of the bowl: lining, then fusible stabilizer, then ultra-firm stabilizer, then bowl fabric. Press with steam.

3. Cut a strip of bias for binding 1½″ x 21″ (3.8 x 53.3cm). Pin around the bottom of the bowl. Trim length if needed, then press the seams.

4. Sew along the edge, following the shape. Sew the seam allowance with blind stitches.

5. Press the seam allowance and blind-stitch, following the shape.

6. Cut one piece of bowl fabric, one piece of stabilizer, one piece of fleece, and one piece of lining, each 3¼″ x 21″ (8.3 x 53.3cm). Make a sandwich: bowl fabric, then fleece, then stabilizer, then lining. Press with steam.

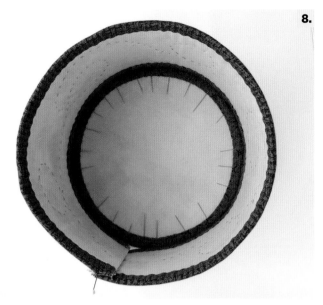

7. With a pastel pencil, draw the design that you will hand- or machine-quilt, then quilt all layers.

8. Cut two strips of binding, 1½" x 21" (3.8 x 53.3cm). Bind both long sides and pin the ends together.

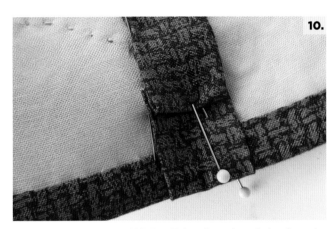

10. Cut a 7¾" x 2" (19.7 x 5.1cm) strip of the bowl fabric. Press under ½" (1.3cm) to the wrong side along each of the long sides. Remove pins from the bottom of the bowl. Pin the strip to cover the connecting stitches on both sides of the bowl; blind-stitch in place.

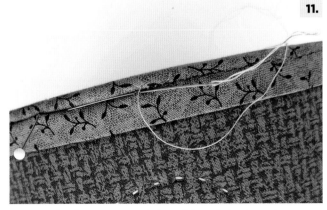

9. Trim the edges and secure them with whipstitch.

11. Pin the bottom and the side of the bowl together; blind-stitch.

13. Insert the seam allowance at the top of the paws. Gently fill with stuffing.

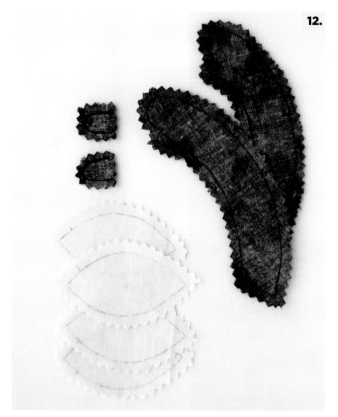

12. Fold the bear fabric with right sides together. Trace, pin, and sew the paws and ears, leaving openings at the bottom. Cut with a ¼″ (0.6cm) seam allowance. Clip the curve where the thumb meets the rest of the paw. Turn these pieces right sides out and press. Refer to steps 1–8 in the Stuffed Ornament project (pages 46–47) for instructions on making the bear's head.

14. Pin the arms on each side of the bowl, coming toward the front, to look as if they're holding the bowl; blind-stitch.

15. Pin the bear's head in place. Blind-stitch along the front and the back edge.

16. Wrap the scarf around the bear's neck.

Gift Box

Wrapping presents can bring just as much joy as giving them, and this small box is perfect for tiny surprises. Add a loop on top, and you have an adorable tree ornament. And if you have the time and patience to sew twenty-four of these boxes, you will have a unique Advent calendar!

YOU WILL NEED:

- Pencil and water-soluble marker
- Cotton yarn and fabric scraps
- Stiletto and eyelets
- Sewing needles, thread, and pins

- Sharp scissors and pinking shears
- Fabric, 17" x 6½" (43.2 x 16.5cm)
- Ultra-firm stabilizer, 6" x 8" (15.2 x 20.3cm)

- Lightweight two-sided fusible web, 6" x 8" (15.2 x 20.3cm)
- Two-sided fusible stabilizer, 6" x 8" (15.2 x 20.3cm)
- Metal snaps or buttons and elastic for closure (optional)

Templates on page 83.

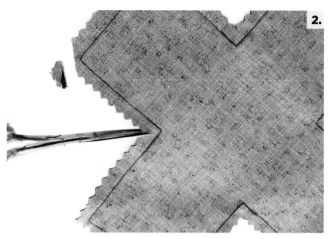

1. Trace the box template onto the ultra-firm stabilizer and cut with no seam allowance. Trace the template onto the lightweight two-sided fusible web and cut with no seam allowance. Press the pieces together.

2. Fold the fabric twice and trace the box template. Sew along the shape, leaving an opening. Cut with a ¼" (0.6cm) seam allowance. Cut the corners. Clip the inside corners.

3. Remove the paper from the fusible web.

4. Turn the fabric right sides out and press. Insert the box base.

5. Place your fabric scraps on the two-sided fusible stabilizer and press through parchment paper. Trace the desired templates onto the fabric scraps.

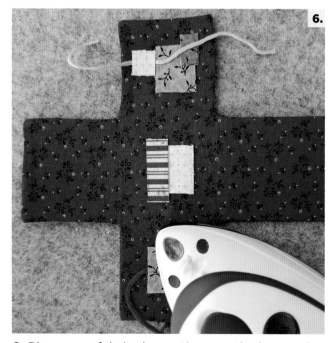

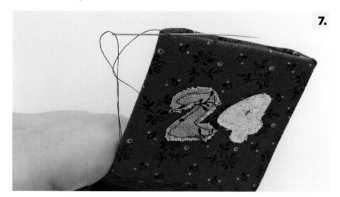

6. Place your fabric decorations on the box and press with steam. Sew each decorative element, following its shape.

7. Turn the seam allowance inside. Press and blind-stitch the opening.

8. Choose one of the following options for closing the box.

Gift Box Options

Make the two holes at the same time with a stiletto as shown. Clip the holes with scissors if needed to fit the eyelets. Insert an eyelet shaft through each hole. Use a hammer to crush the eyelet shafts over the fabric.

Pin the sides of the box together and blind-stitch. Pull yarn through both eyelets and make a bow.

Finished gift box with bow closure.

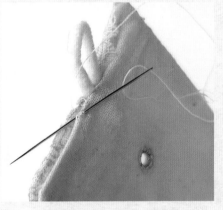

Sew on a button as shown.

Make an elastic loop and insert it into the opening. Blind-stitch.

Finished gift box with button and loop closure.

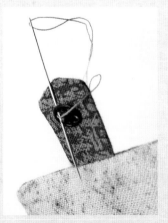

Sew on one half of a metal snap closure.

Make a small flap and insert it into the opening. Blind-stitch.

Attach the other half of the snap at the end of the flap with several stitches.

Finished gift box with snap closure.

Treat Tray

There is no such a thing as having too many trays—especially when they hold wonderful treats. Decorate this tray's borders with evergreen garland, load it up with as many cookies as it can hold, and enjoy with some hot chocolate!

YOU WILL NEED:

- Pastel pencil
- Long needle
- Eight pieces of cord, each 5" (12.7cm) long
- Sewing needles, thread, and pins
- Two different-colored fabrics, one piece each, 8½" x 8½" (21.6 x 21.6cm)
- Assortment of fabric scraps
- Two pieces two-sided fusible stabilizer, 8½" x 8½" (21.6 x 21.6cm)
- Two pieces ultra-firm stabilizer, 8½" x 8½" (21.6 x 21.6cm)
- Parchment paper
- Sharp scissors and pinking shears

1. Place your fabric scraps on the two-sided fusible stabilizer and press through parchment paper.

2. Trace and cut the decorative elements (see Decorations for Gift Box templates on page 83) from the fabric scraps.

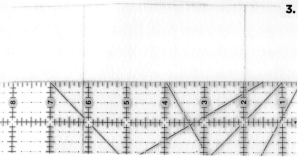

3. To make the base of the tray, cut two 8" x 8" (20.3 x 20.3cm) squares of both the firm stabilizer and the fusible stabilizer. Mark in 2" (5.1cm) from each side so that the sides of the tray are 2" (5.1cm) high and the bottom of the tray is 4" x 4" (10.2 x 10.2cm). Press both layers of stabilizer through parchment paper.

4. Cut one piece each of two different-colored fabrics, 8½" x 8½" (21.6 x 21.6cm). Put right sides together and sew with ¼" (0.6cm) seam allowance, leaving an opening. Clip the corners of the square.

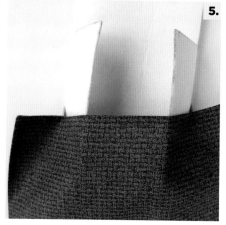

5. Turn the fabric right sides out and press. Cut a 2" x 2" (5.1 x 5.1cm) square from each corner of the tray base. Insert the base into the fabric casing, fusible side up.

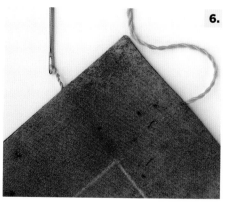

6. With a pastel pencil, mark the 4" x 4" (10.2 x 10.2cm) tray bottom on the inside of the tray. Make a knot on one end of one of the pieces of cord (see page 13). Pull it through the seam at one corner. Make a knot on the other end of the cord. Repeat for all corners.

Template on page 84.

7. Blind-stitch the opening at each corner.

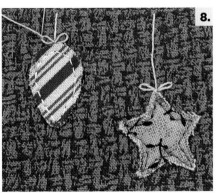

8. Press the decorative elements in place with steam, then sew around the shape of each decoration. Make some long stitches and looped stitches to give the appearance of ornaments hanging from the sides of the tray.

9. Stitch around the bottom square and fold up the sides. Make a bow with the cord at each corner.

Mug Rug

Whimsy, Brownie, and Honey have a new adventure: a tea party! Our three bear friends add some fun and a decorative touch to teatime. These 6" (15.2cm) square mug rugs make perfect coasters for teacups or coffee mugs, and they can be easily enlarged to make placemats. Following are the step-by-step instructions for the Whimsy (panda) block as an example, but you can adapt these instructions to make any of the three bear blocks (pages 64–72).

6"(15.2cm) QUILT BLOCK
SCALE 1:1

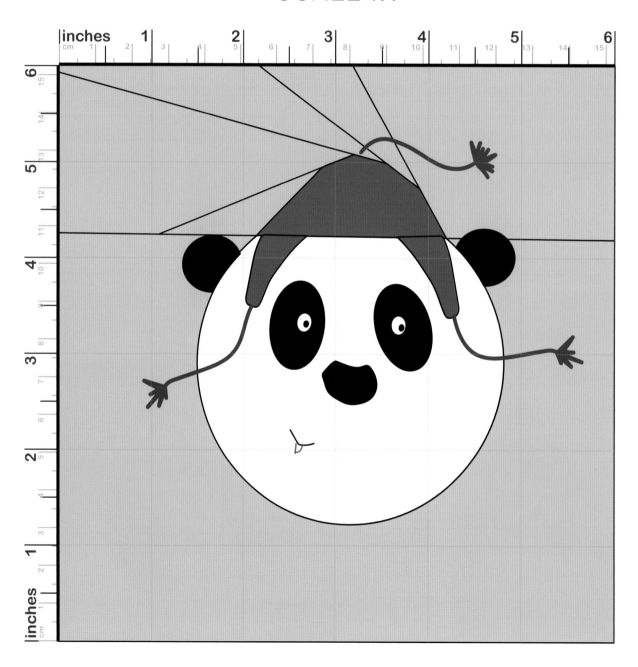

Templates on
pages 85–87.

1

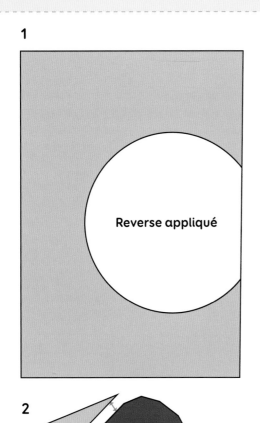

Reverse appliqué

Template on page 85.

4

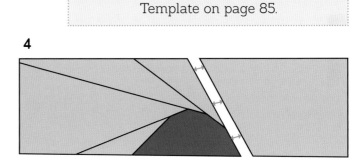

5

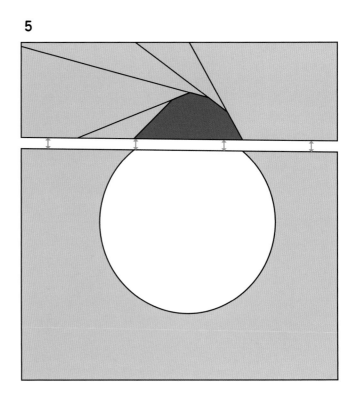

2

3

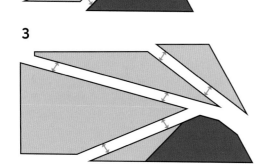

Constructing the Block

You will appliqué and reverse appliqué most of the details on the bear block for this project, using blind stitching by hand (or by machine). The basic process is to cut the piece to be appliquéd, roll the edges under, then sew with blind stitches. If you prefer, you can use the raw-edge appliqué method instead (see Three Presents Tag with Raw-Edge Appliqué on page 44).

1. Gather your fabric scraps for the bear block (see materials list on page 6). Place the fabric for the bear's head so that the right side is against the back side of the background fabric.

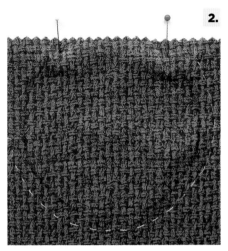

2. Cut the silhouette of the head and transfer it with a water-soluble marker to the right side of the background fabric. Mark the ears, then pin the fabrics. Sew with a running stitch. For easy thread removal, do not make a knot.

3. Carefully cut out the design inside of your marked line, cutting only the top layer of the fabric and leaving a ¼" (0.6cm) seam allowance. Then clip the curves, being careful not to clip past the traced line.

4. Turn the seam allowance under along the traced line and blind-stitch.

5. Trace the face details (ears, nose, eyes). Note: When working with dark fabric, I recommend using a white pastel pencil because it makes visible marks that are also easy to remove. Cut the pieces out with a ¼" (0.6cm) seam allowance.

6. Turn the seams of the ears to the wrong side of the background fabric. Pin the ears, right sides together with the face fabric, the places where you marked previously. Continue blind-stitching.

7.

7. Cut extra fabric from the wrong side if needed.

8.

8. Take out the basting thread. Pin the hat pieces in place. Add the top patchwork pieces of background fabric as shown in illustrations 2–5.

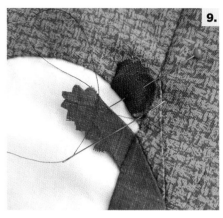

9.

9. Trace the ear with a water-soluble marker on the right side of the background fabric, then lay the ear in place and pin. Blind-stitch, following the shape and turning the seam allowance under as you stitch. Do the same with the other ear.

10.

10. Appliqué the rest of the face details and hat in the same way. Remove the traced lines with a damp cotton swab.

11. Trim the block to 6″ (15.2cm) square and iron it.

TIP: You can easily mix appliqué techniques when constructing the bear's head by turning under the seam allowance around the face and making the ears with raw-edge appliqué.

Making the Mug Rug

2.

1. Place the one-sided fusible fleece with the glue side to the wrong side of the block. Press with steam.

2. Stitch the hat details with couching, using a two-color cord (see page 13) as your foundation thread and a single white thread as your working thread. Here's how to do the couching stitch: Place pins in a line where you want your foundation thread to lie. Bring the foundation thread up through the back of the fabric at the top of the hat, then place the foundation thread along the line of pins.

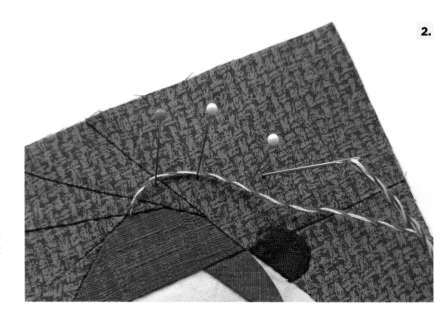

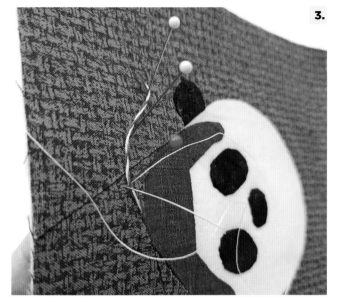

3. Make a loose stitch and secure the foundation thread at the back of the fabric. Bring the couching thread up through the back of the fabric near the point where the foundation thread meets the hat, then take a short straight stitch over the foundation thread. Re-emerge a short distance along the foundation thread and take another short straight stitch over it with the couching thread.

4. Remove the pins. Secure the couching thread at the back of the fabric. Stitch the other hat details in the same way.

5. Make several stitches at the end of each two-colored cord to look like fringe.

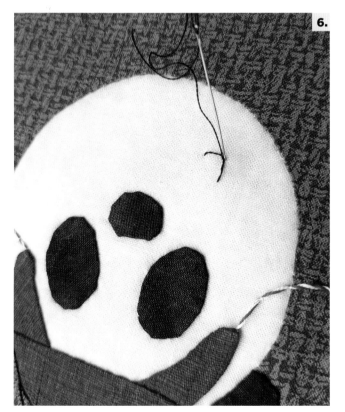

6. Stitch the mouth with black thread and the tongue with red thread.

7. With a water-soluble marker, draw the design that you will hand- or machine-quilt over the block. Place the backing fabric with the wrong side facing in, then quilt all layers. Remove the drawn lines with a damp cotton swab.

8. Pin and blind-stitch along the edge of the 1⅜" x 24" (3.5 x 61cm) bias strip (see page 30) to make the binding. Cut extra bias if needed. Press and blind-stitch.

9. Draw the details (see page 8).

6"(15.2cm) QUILT BLOCK
SCALE 1:1

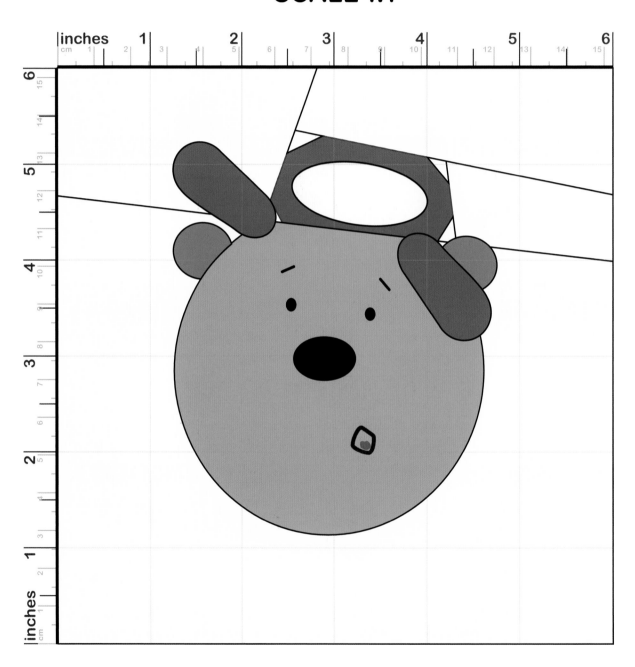

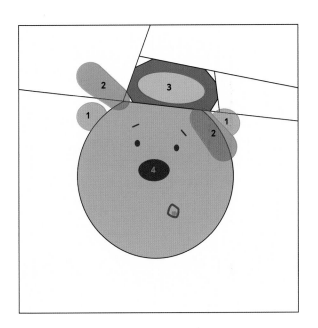

Template on
page 86.

1

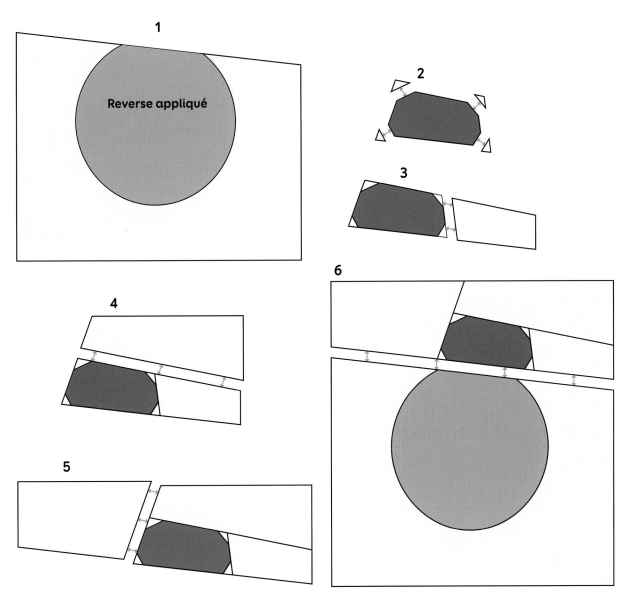

Reverse appliqué

2

3

6

4

5

6"(15.2cm) QUILT BLOCK
SCALE 1:1

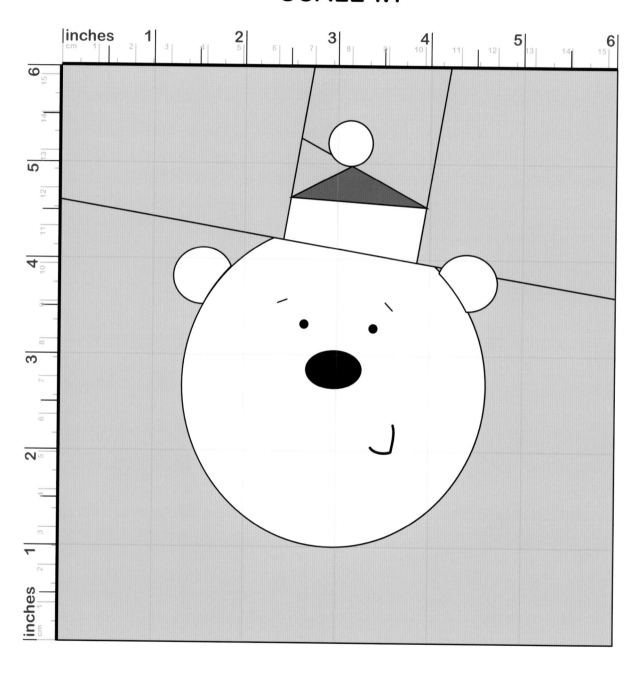

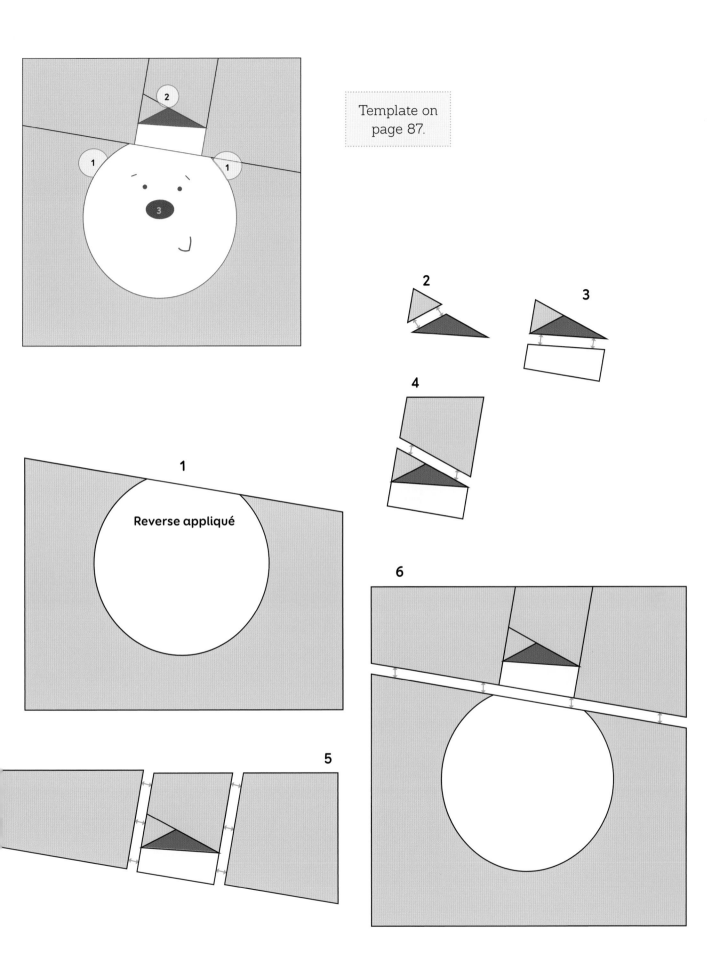

Template on
page 87.

2

3

4

1

Reverse appliqué

6

5

Templates

Photocopy at 100%.

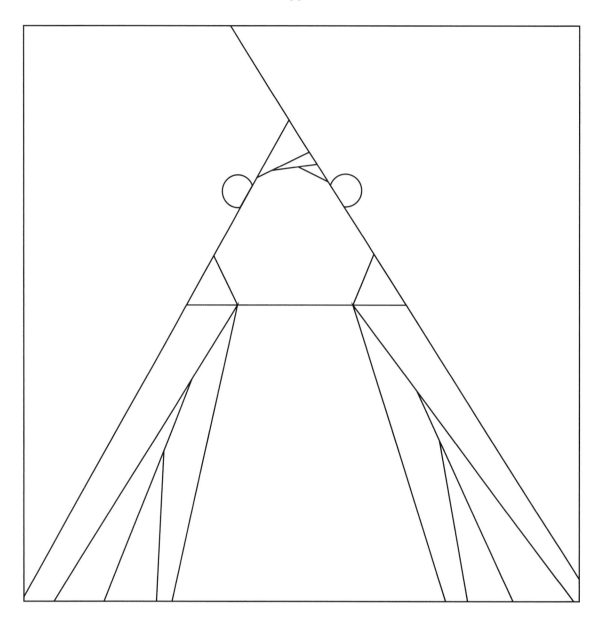

Holly Jolly

Knitted scarf
embellishment

Be Bright

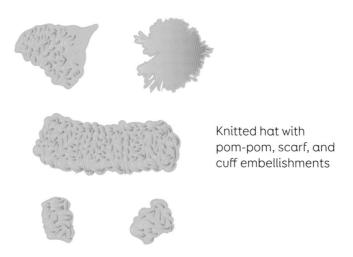

Knitted hat with
pom-pom, scarf, and
cuff embellishments

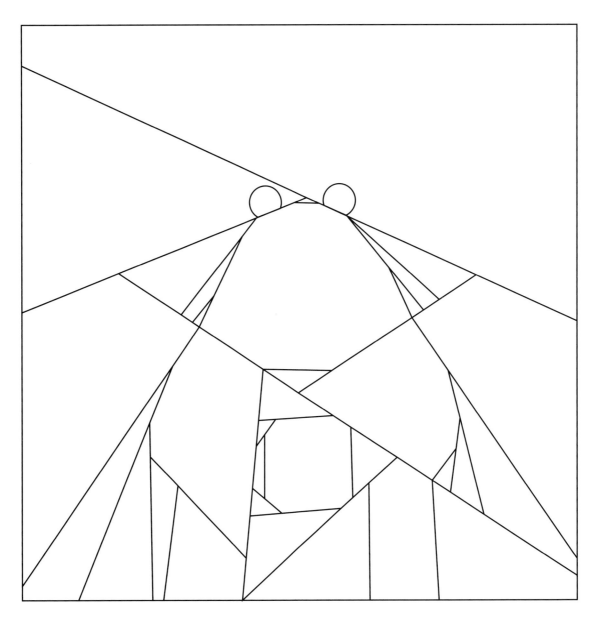

Joyful Wishes

Knitted mitten embellishments

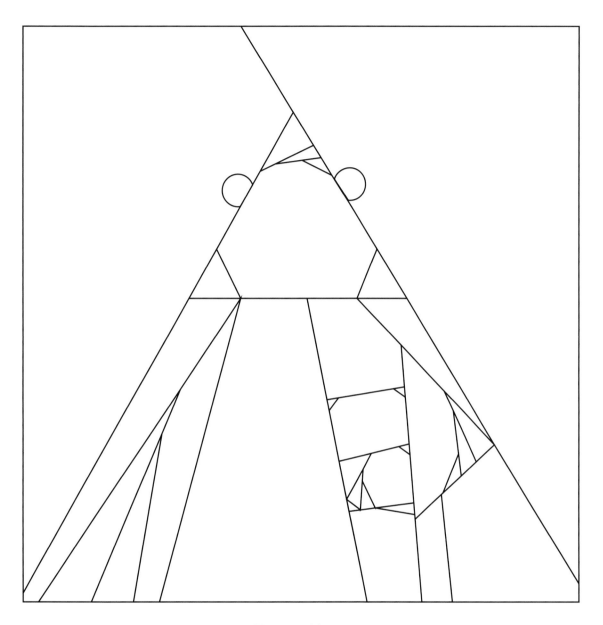

Toasty Hugs

Knitted scarf and
cuff embellishments

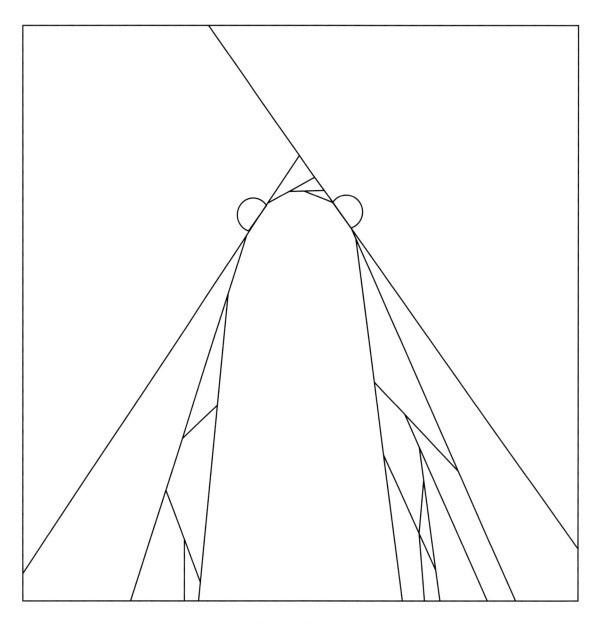

Warm Wishes

Knitted scarf
embellishment

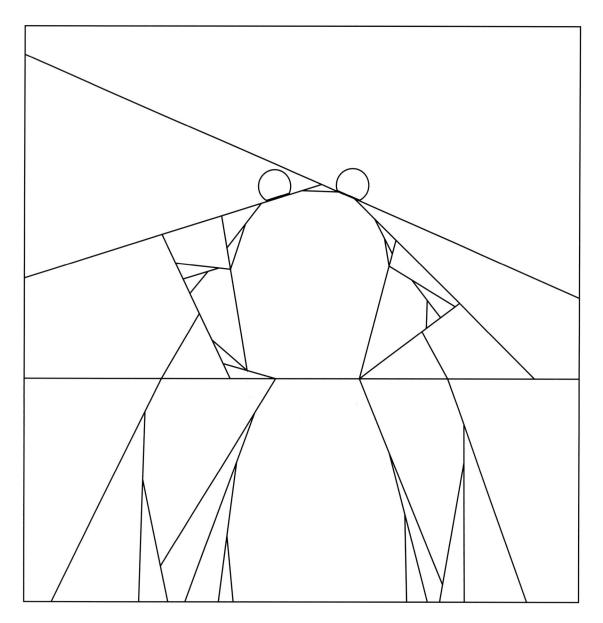

Stay Cozy

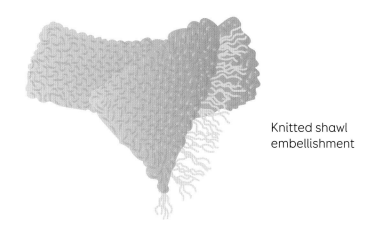

Knitted shawl
embellishment

Gift Tag with Knitted Pom-Pom Hat

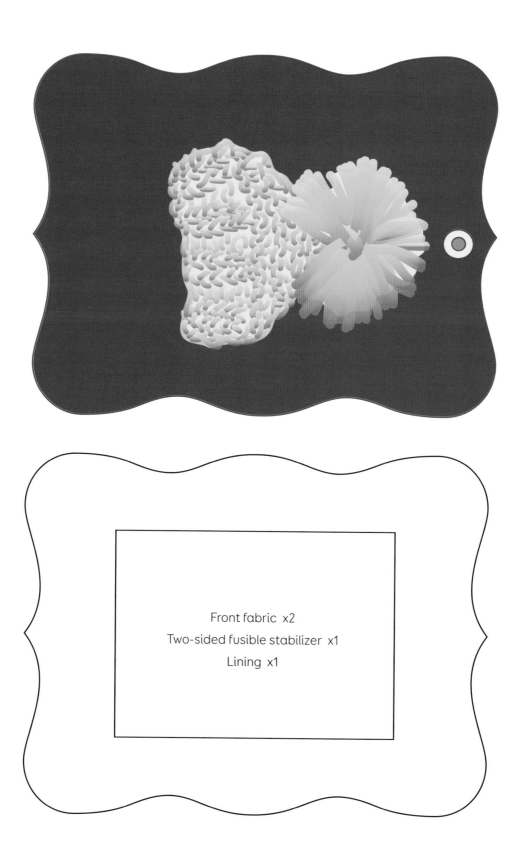

Front fabric x2
Two-sided fusible stabilizer x1
Lining x1

Template from Sewing Cozy Craft Projects © Olaqua Lebandenko and Landauar Publishing

Curly Gift Tag with Knitted Mittens

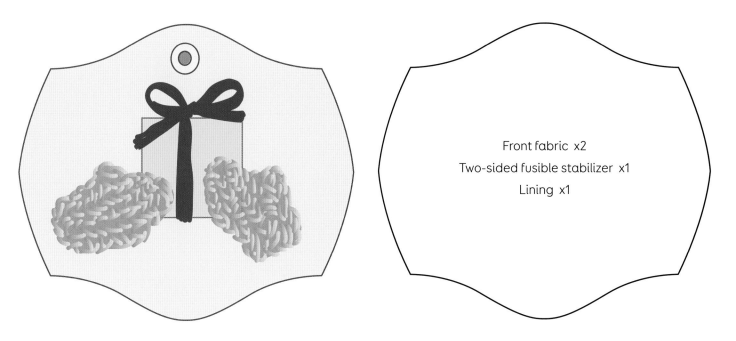

Front fabric x2
Two-sided fusible stabilizer x1
Lining x1

Ornament Gift Tag with Raw-Edge Appliqué

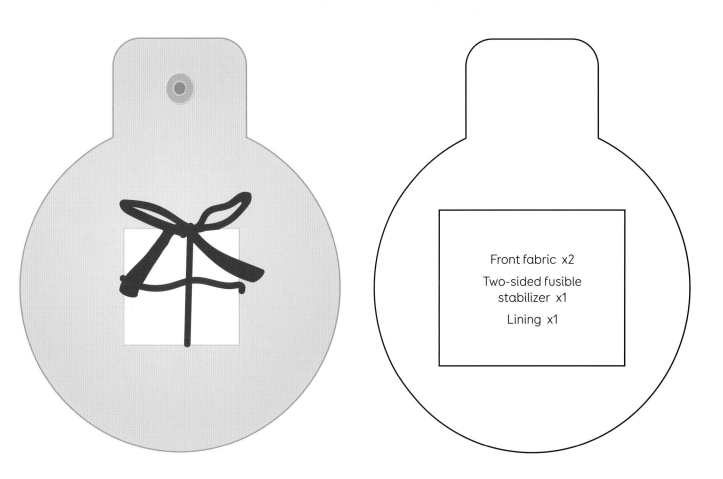

Front fabric x2

Two-sided fusible
stabilizer x1

Lining x1

Present Gift Tag with Raw-Edge Appliqué

Front fabric x2

Two-sided fusible
stabilizer x1

Lining x1

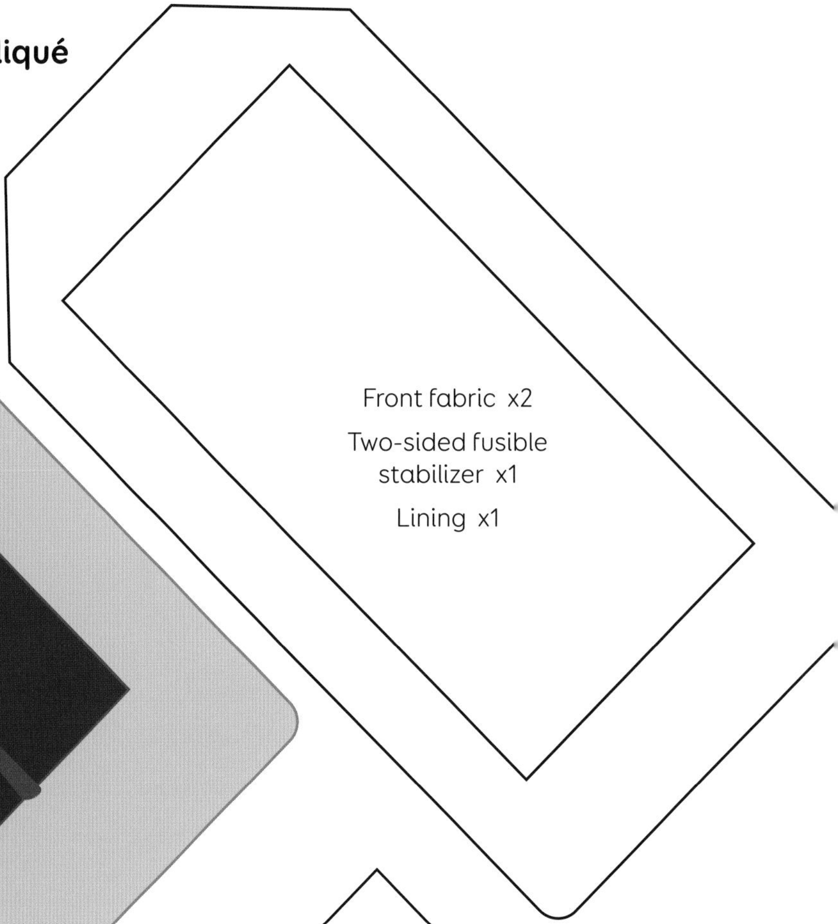

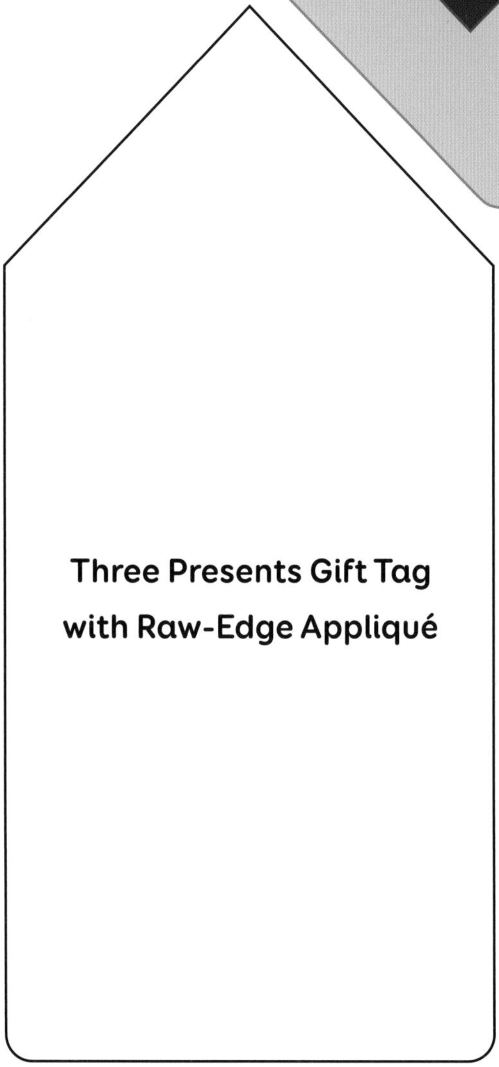

Three Presents Gift Tag
with Raw-Edge Appliqué

Front fabric x2

Two-sided fusible
stabilizer x1

Lining x1

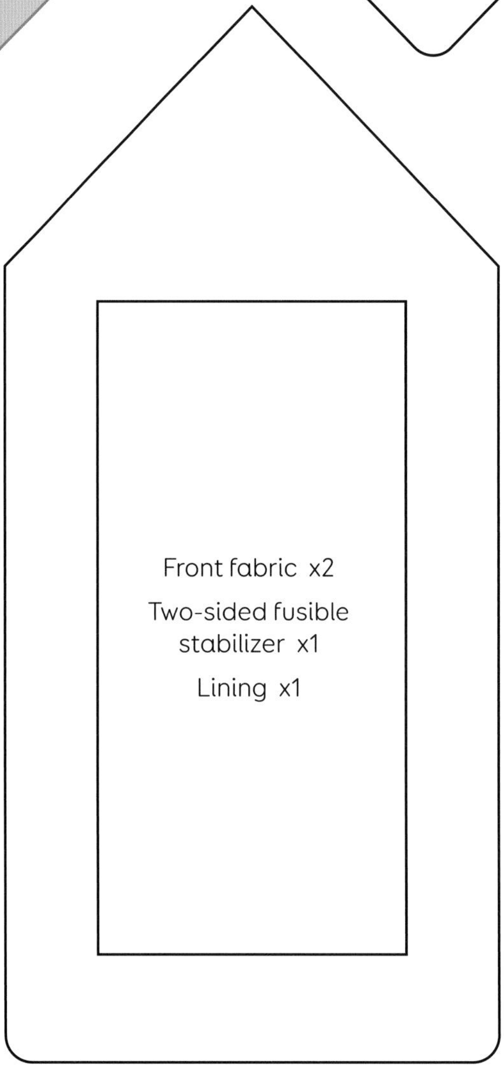

Template from *Sewing Cozy Craft Projects* © Olesya Lebendenko and Landauer Publishing, an imprint of Fox Chapel Publishing Company, Inc.

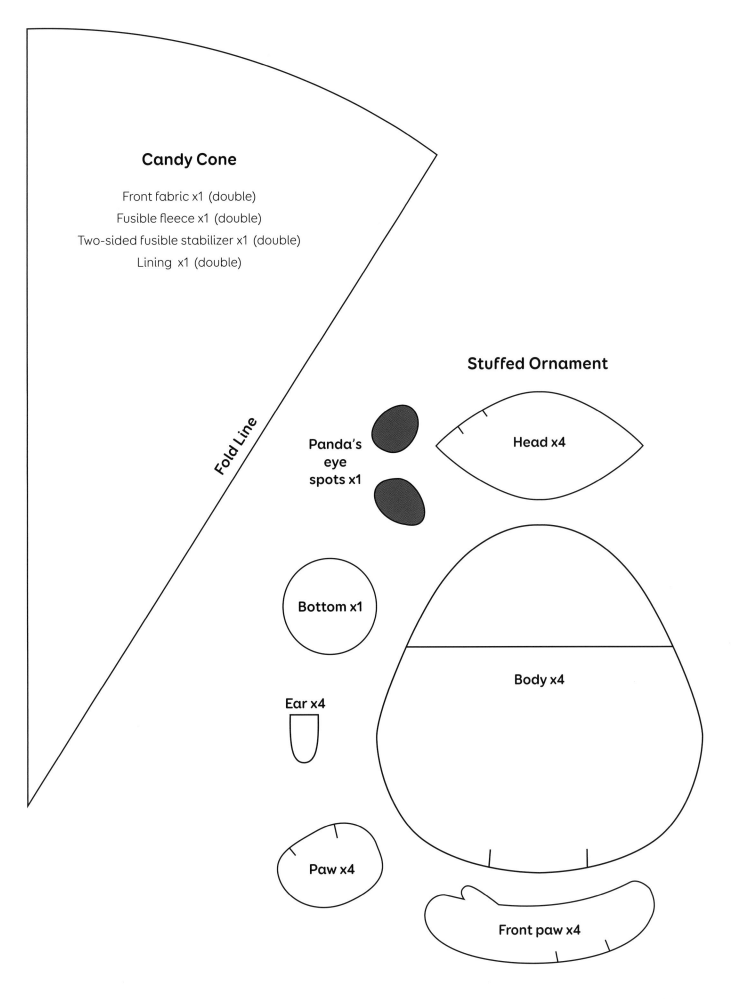

Candy Cone

Front fabric x1 (double)

Fusible fleece x1 (double)

Two-sided fusible stabilizer x1 (double)

Lining x1 (double)

Fold Line

Stuffed Ornament

Panda's eye spots x1

Head x4

Bottom x1

Body x4

Ear x4

Paw x4

Front paw x4

Candy Cone and Cookie Bowl

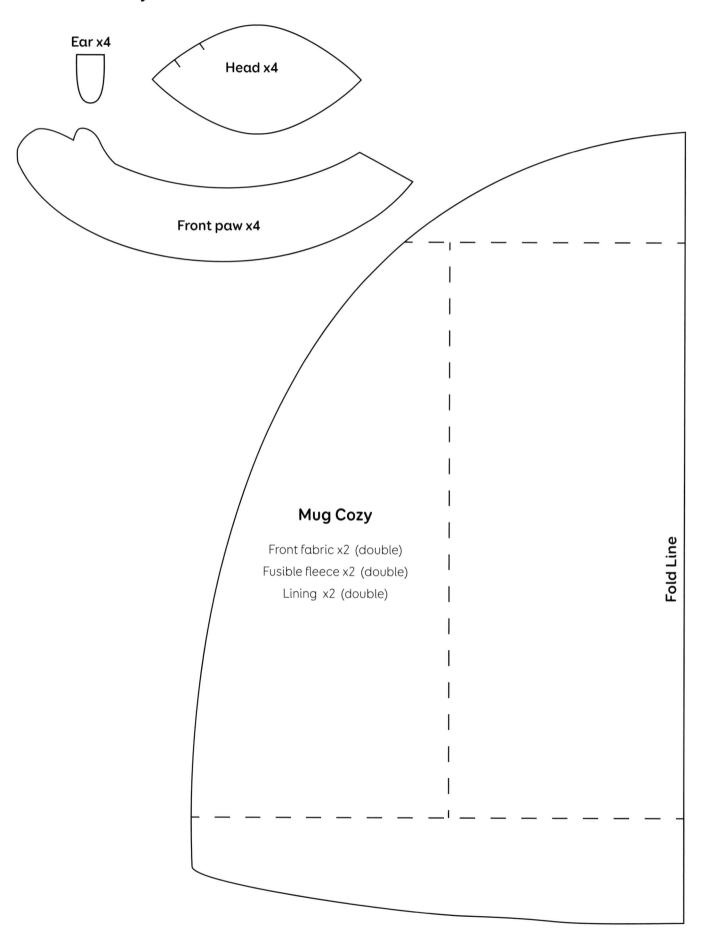

Ear x4

Head x4

Front paw x4

Mug Cozy

Front fabric x2 (double)

Fusible fleece x2 (double)

Lining x2 (double)

Fold Line

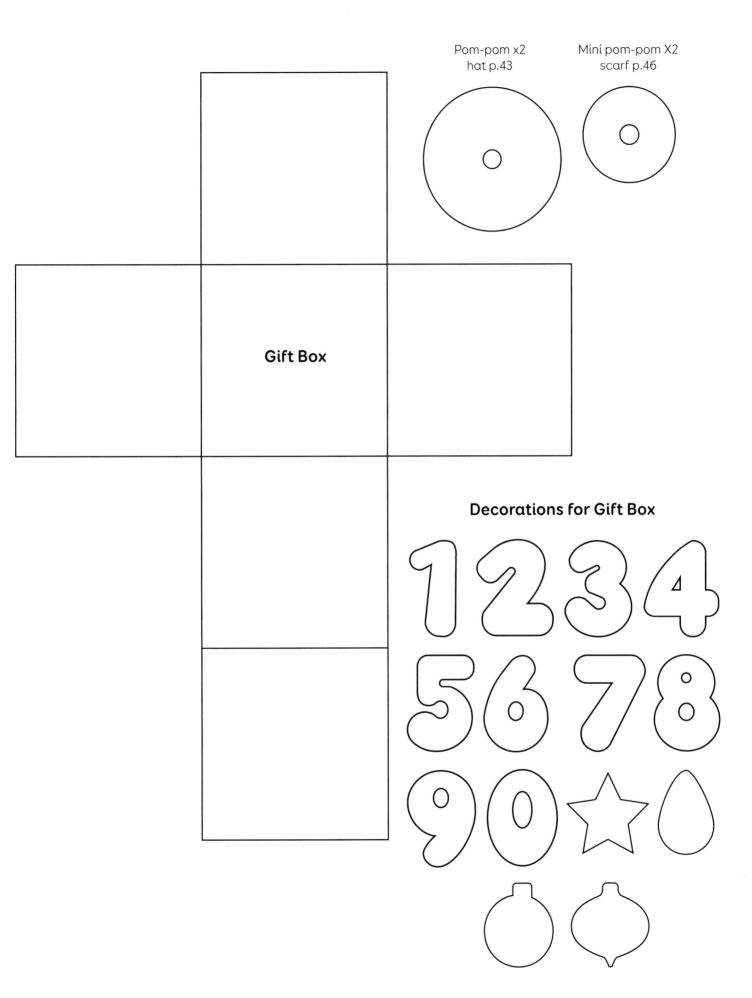

Pom-pom x2
hat p.43

Mini pom-pom X2
scarf p.46

Gift Box

Decorations for Gift Box

Treat Tray

Whimsy Mug Rug

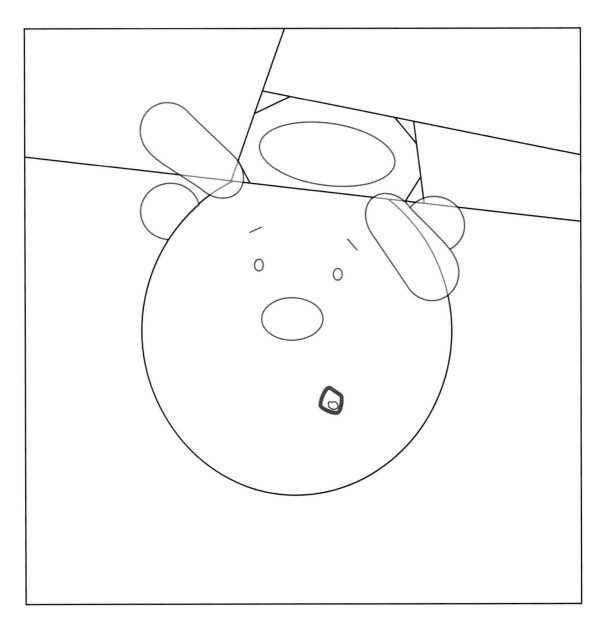

Brownie Mug Rug

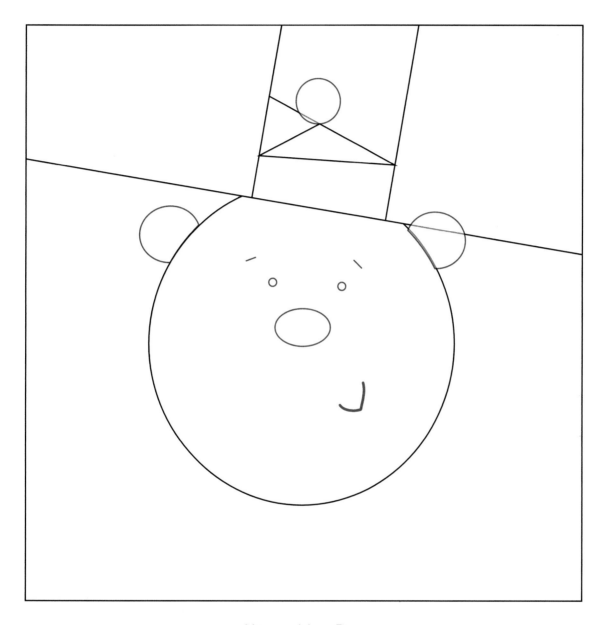

Honey Mug Rug

Index

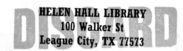

About the Author

Author **Olesya Lebedenko** is an artist from Ukraine living in Canada, where she works and creates modern template designs. She is a teacher, designer, quilter, doll maker, author, magazine contributor, and entrepreneur as the founder and owner of Olesya Lebedenko Design. Her work has been featured in American, Canadian, and Ukrainian publications, she has written countless tutorials and articles, and she has led hundreds of workshops all over Europe and Canada.

Olesya is a professional member of the International Quilt Association and the Canadian Quilters' Association. In 2020, she became a BERNINA Canada Ambassador. To learn more about Olesya Lebedenko and to view her work, visit her website (*www.olesya-l-design.com*), her Instagram (*@olesyalebedenkodesign*), and her Etsy shop (*www.etsy.com/shop/ OlesyaLebedenkoDsgn*).